Fourth Position Study Method

for Cello

by Cassia Harvey

CHP347
©2018 C. Harvey Publications All Rights Reserved.
www.charveypublications.com
www.learnstrings.com

Table of Contents

First finger	4
Second finger	11
Fourth finger	16
Third finger	22
Review notes in fourth position	30
Slurs	31
Mid-string harmonics	38
Extending back to a flat	48
Extending forward to a sharp	58
Double stops	68
Tone and vibrato	70
Shifting back 1/2 step	72
Shifting forward 1/2 step	73

Fourth Position on the Cello Fingerboard

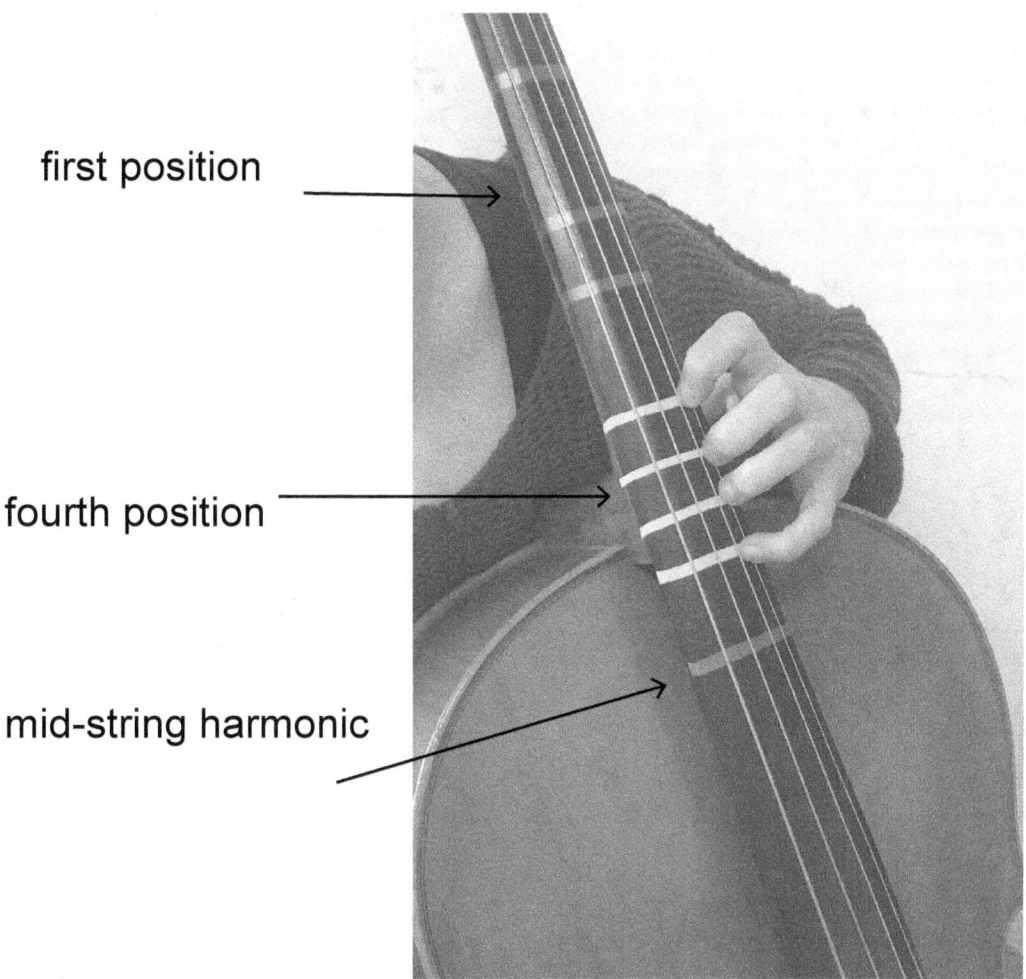

Fourth Position is a specific place to put your fingers on the cello.

Cellists play in fourth position for a variety of reasons, including reaching new notes, avoiding open strings, and making playing less awkward. To reach fourth position, your hand will leave first position and **shift** (move to a new place.)

In this book, the combination of a finger number and the note under it indicates a shift.

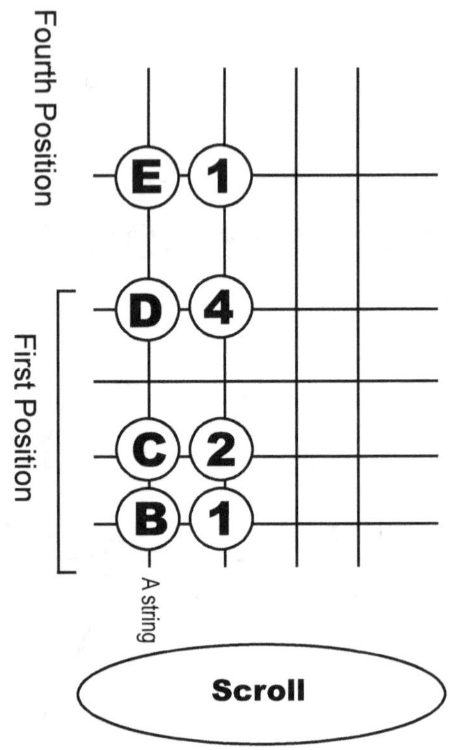

See page 3 for a picture of fourth position on the cello.

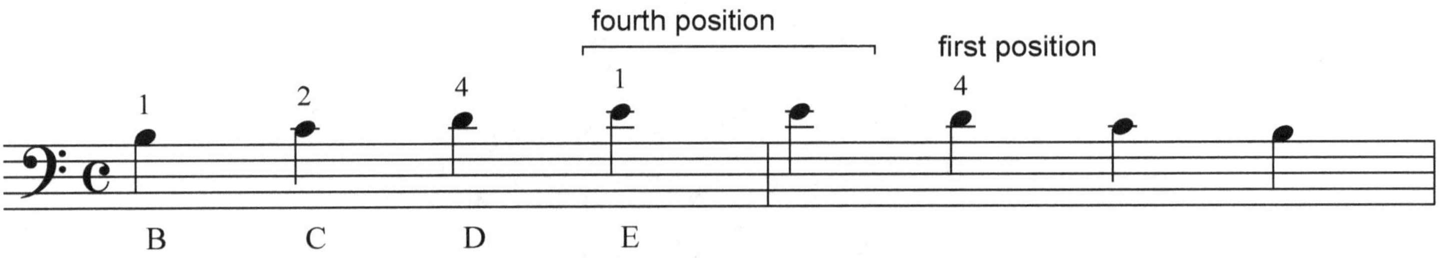

If you put a different finger on the note E, you will be in a different position.
In this book, we will be playing in first and fourth positions.

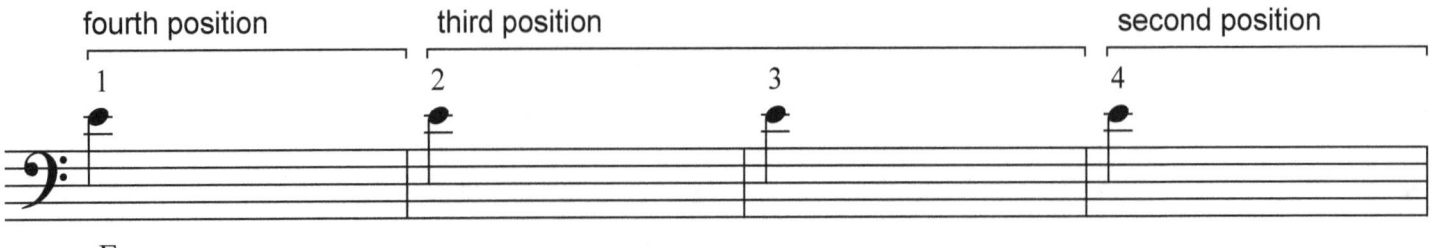

Fourth Position on the Other Strings

Note:

Roman Numerals below the notes tell you which string to play on.

I = A string
II = D string
III = G string
IV = C string

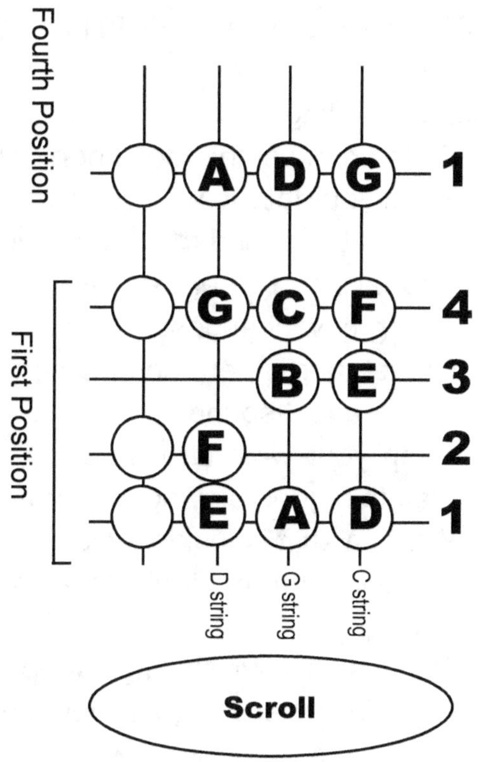

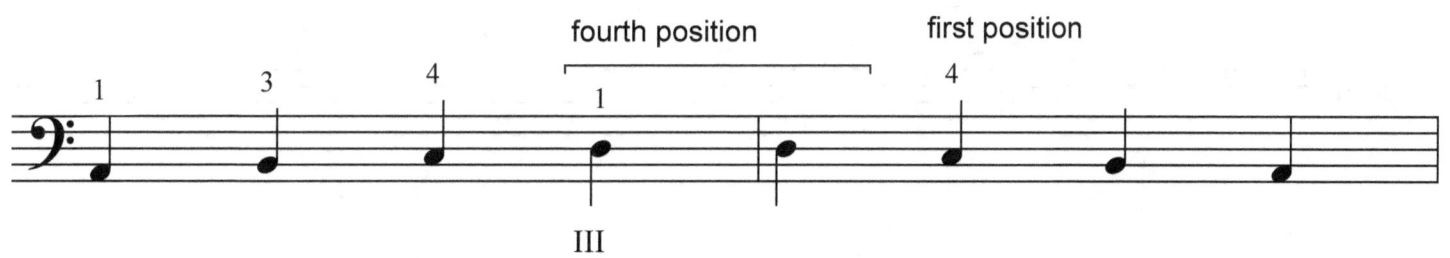

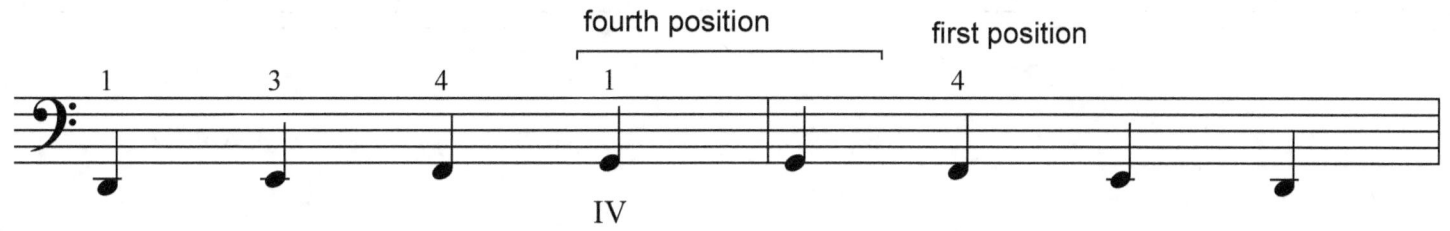

©2018 C. Harvey Publications. All Rights Reserved.

Shifting is moving your (left) hand to another place on the cello.

Tips for Shifting
- Slide on the string; don't hop or jump off of the string to get to the new position.
- Bring your thumb with you (on the neck of the cello) as you shift.
- Expect the sound to be a bit squeaky and imperfect at first; it will improve as you shift more.
- Squeaks and other extra sounds will disappear as you get used to timing your shifts to happen during bow changes.
- Curve your fingers and play on the tip of your fingers as you shift to move smoothly and get the cleanest sound.
- Keep your wrist straight and your arm out to the side (away from your body) as you shift; maintain good playing posture.
- When a shift is inside a slur, some sliding sound might happen. How much sliding sound you make is more controllable as you gain experience shifting and can regulate the speed of the shift.
- Don't rush your shifting. Keep your hand relaxed as you calmly move to the next position. Learning where to go is more important than getting there quickly, especially at the beginning.

Practice shifting to E in fourth position on the A string.

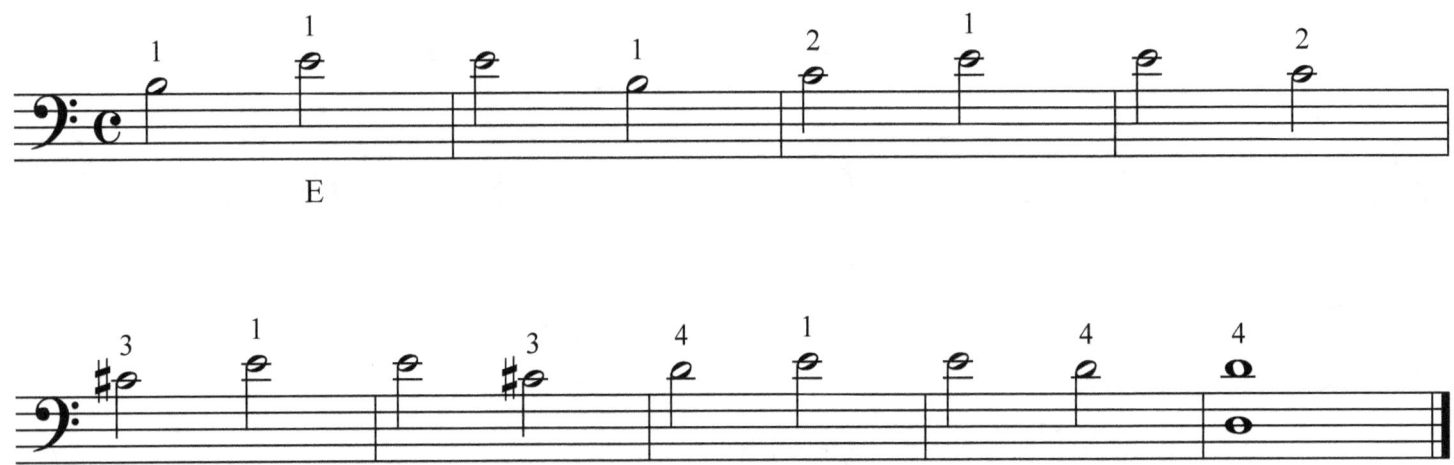

Practice shifting to fourth position on the other strings.

Note: Stay in position until a finger number tells you to shift again.

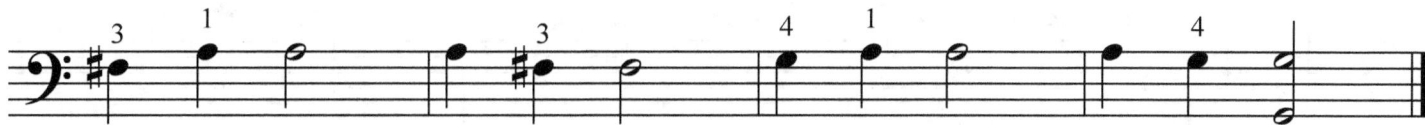

Note: A review of how Roman Numerals are used in this book is on page 5.

A String Shifting Study

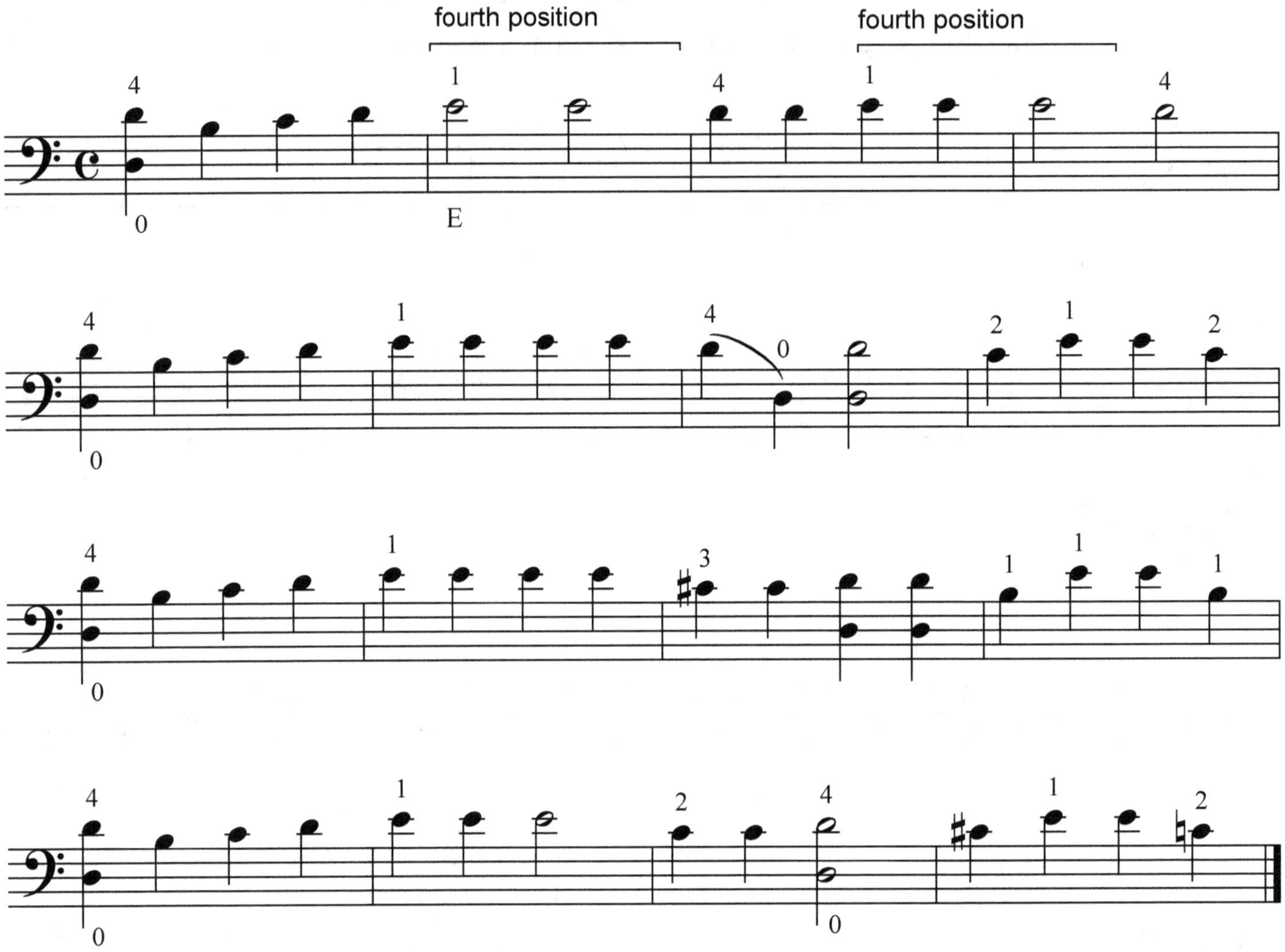

Form Tips

- Keep your left arm out to the side, with the elbow only slightly sloped down from your shoulder.
- Curve the fingers of the left hand as you shift; play on the tips of the fingers.
- Don't forget to slide your thumb with your hand, under the neck, as you shift.
- Move the bow slightly closer to the bridge; in general, the bow should be around the middle of the space between the fingerboard and bridge. This gives you a slightly longer string to make vibrate and can result in better sound.

Across Strings in Fourth Position

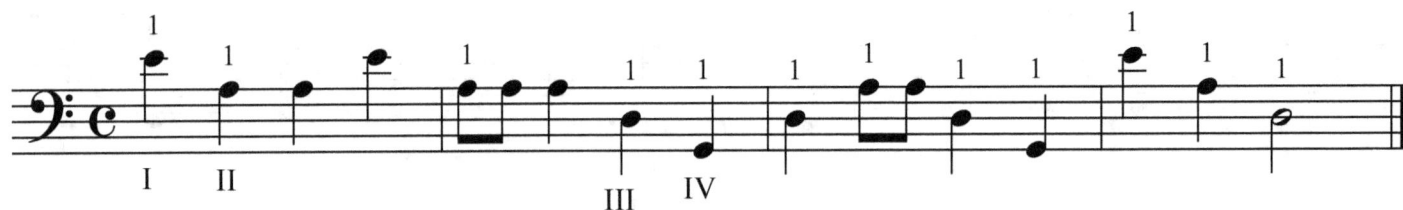

©2018 C. Harvey Publications. All Rights Reserved.

Fourth Position Study Method for Cello

Auld Lang Syne Exercise

Auld Lang Syne

Trad., arr. Harvey

The sharps or flats in the key signature will be listed here, at the beginning of each piece.

F#

©2018 C. Harvey Publications. All Rights Reserved.

All Through the Night Exercise

Variations on 'All Through the Night'

Trad., arr. Harvey

Second Finger F♮ on the A string

Note: the spaces between your fingers will be slightly smaller in fourth position than they are in first position.

Second Finger B♭ on the D string

Folk Melody

Harvey

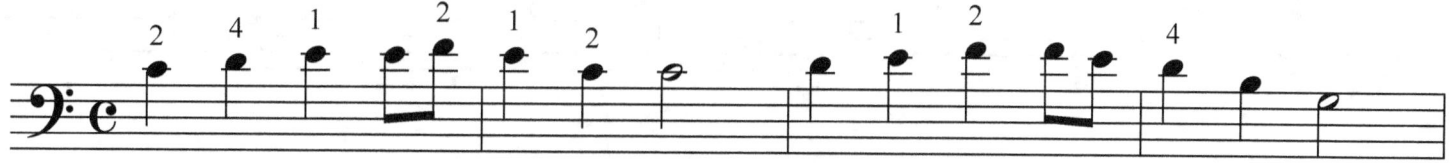

©2018 C. Harvey Publications. All Rights Reserved.

Rigadoon

Purcell, arr. Harvey

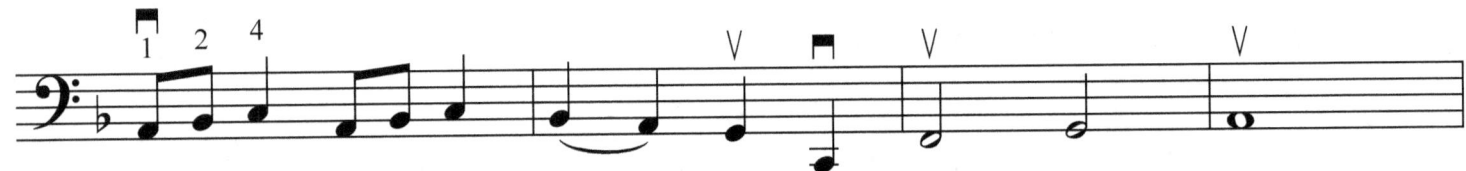

Across Strings in Fourth Position

©2018 C. Harvey Publications. All Rights Reserved.

Fourth Position Study Method for Cello

Exercise for The Blue Bells of Scotland

The Blue Bells of Scotland

Trad., arr. Harvey

©2018 C. Harvey Publications. All Rights Reserved.

Second Finger E♭ on the G string

Second Finger A♭ on the C string

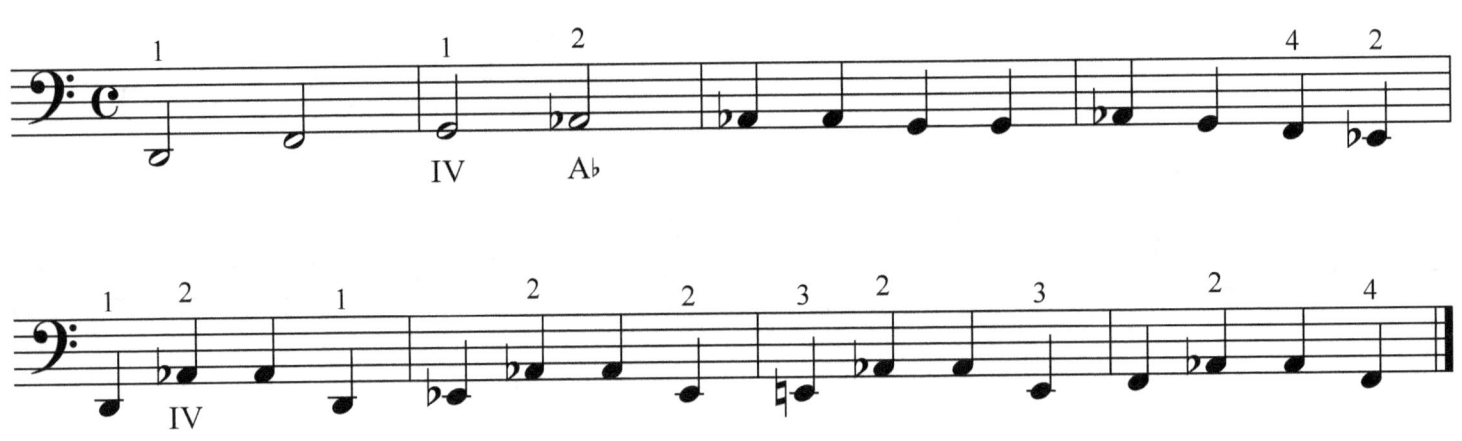

Across Strings in Fourth Position

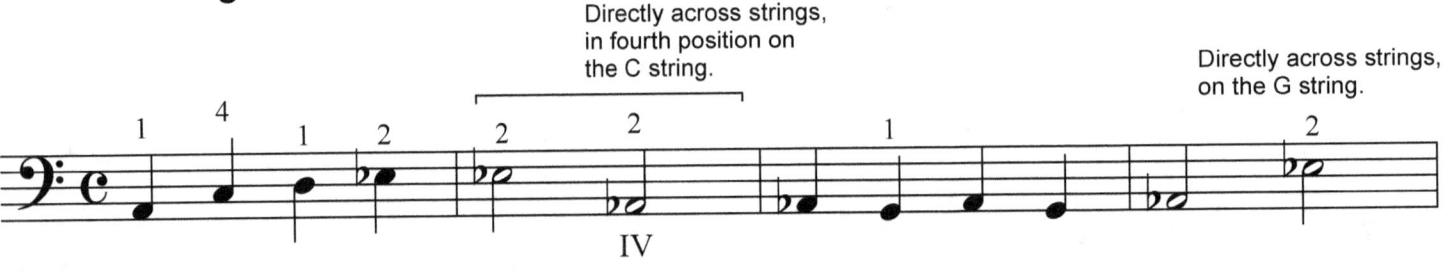

©2018 C. Harvey Publications. All Rights Reserved.

Exercise for The Minstrel Boy

B♭, E♭
A♭

The Minstrel Boy

Trad., arr. Harvey

B♭, E♭
A♭

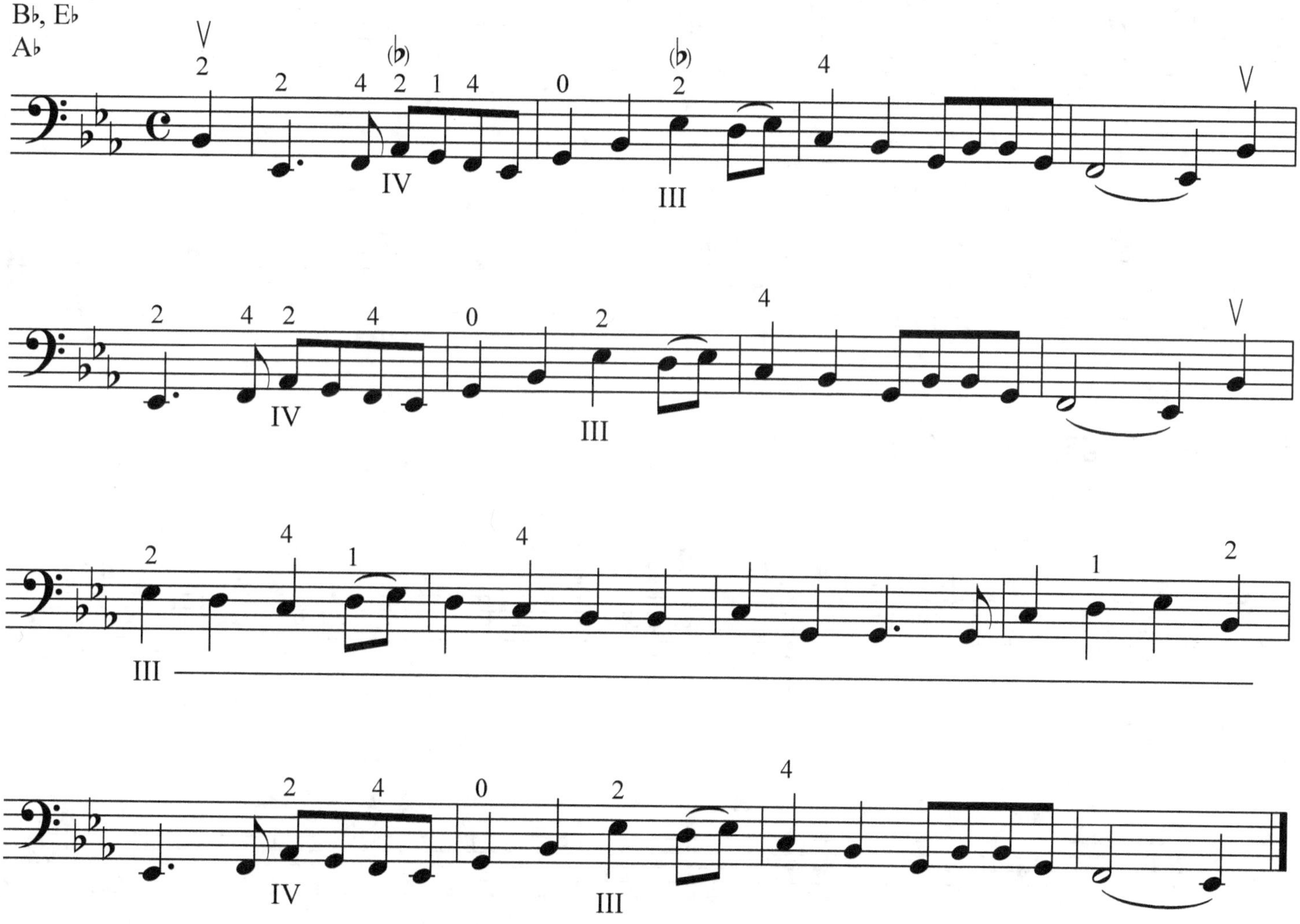

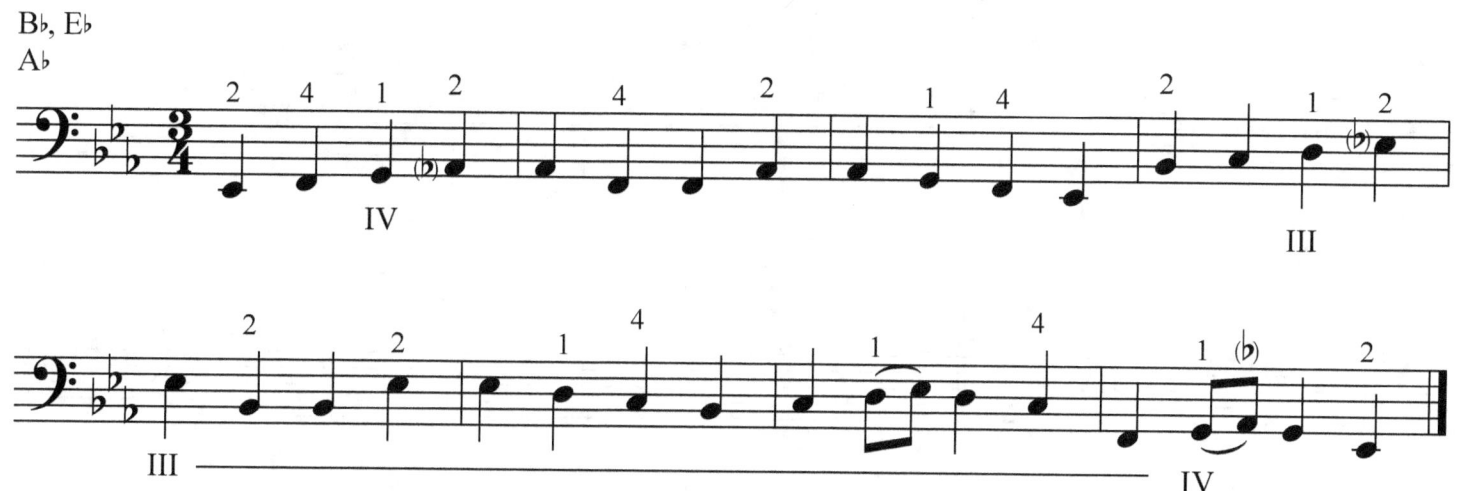

Fourth Finger G on the A string

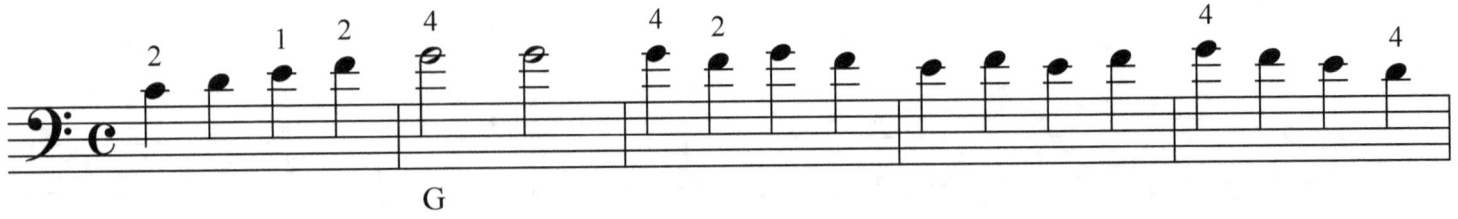

Fourth Finger C on the D string

Across Strings in Fourth Position

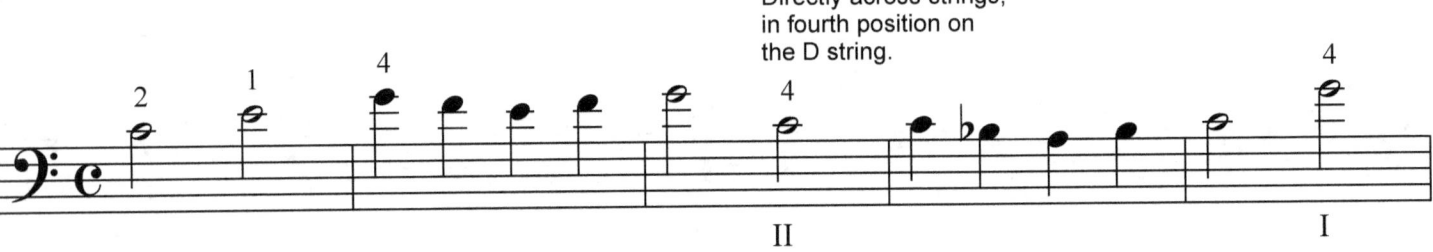

Directly across strings, in fourth position on the D string.

Exercise for Polly Wolly Doodle

Note: When you are already in 4th position use 1st finger to play A on the D string, rather than the open A, so that the tone matches the other notes.

Polly Wolly Doodle

Trad., arr. Harvey

©2018 C. Harvey Publications. All Rights Reserved.

Fourth Finger F on the G string

Fourth Finger B♭ on the C string

Across Strings in Fourth Position

Exercise for The Streets of Laredo

Note: This line tells you to stay on the G string to play the notes after the III.

The Streets of Laredo

Trad., arr. Harvey

Finger Exercise with 2nd Finger

Note: For even faster fingers in fourth position, try the ebook *Fourth Position Finger Exercises for the Cello* (CHPD07).

©2018 C. Harvey Publications. All Rights Reserved.

Fourth Position Study Method for Cello

Exercise for The Golden Vanity

The Golden Vanity

Trad., arr. Harvey

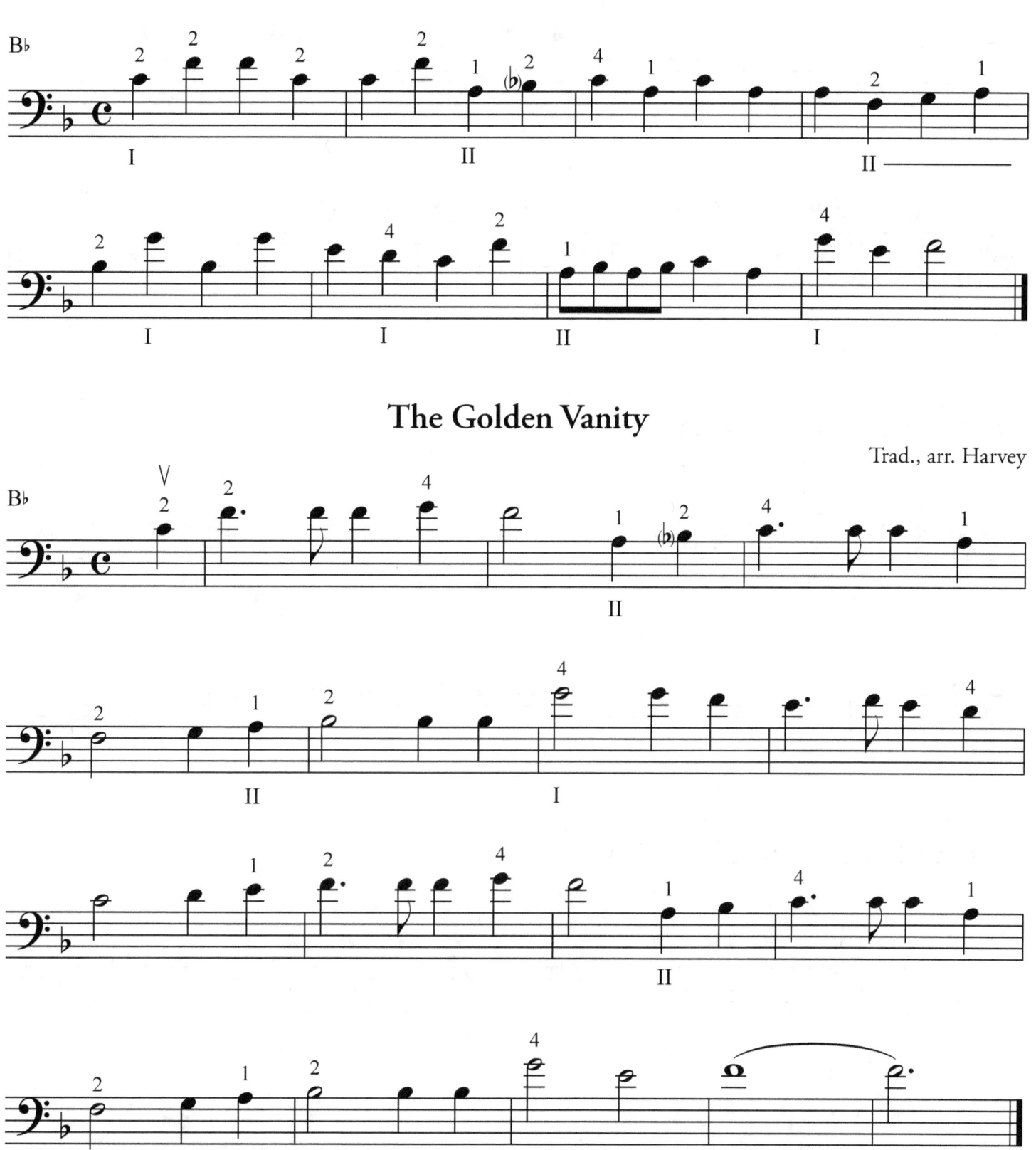

Third Finger F# on the A string

Third Finger B on the D string

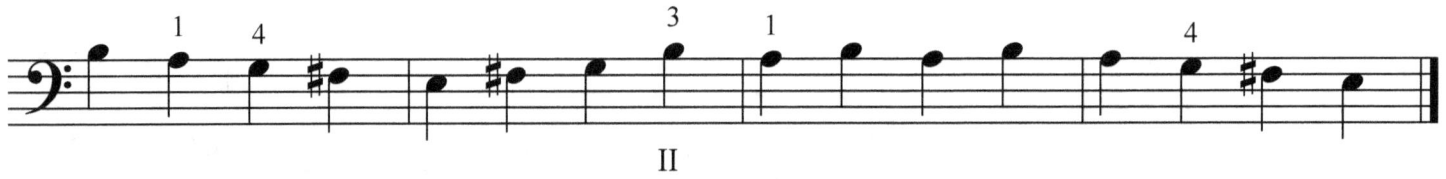

Across Strings in Fourth Position

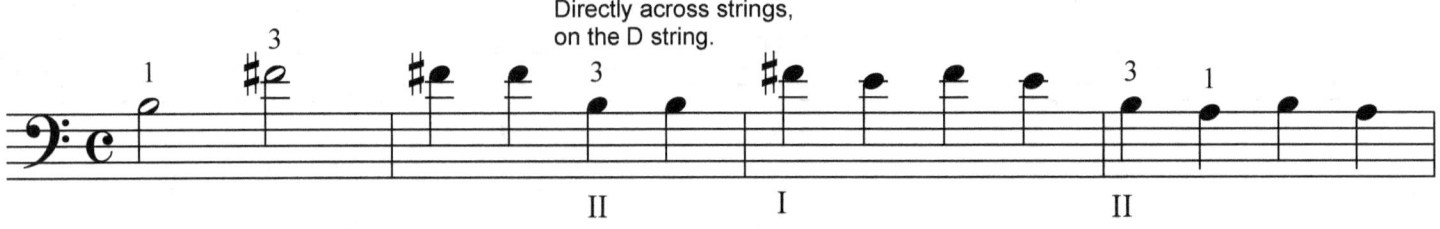

©2018 C. Harvey Publications. All Rights Reserved.

Wraggle Taggle Exercise

The Wraggle-Taggle Gypsies

Trad., arr. Harvey

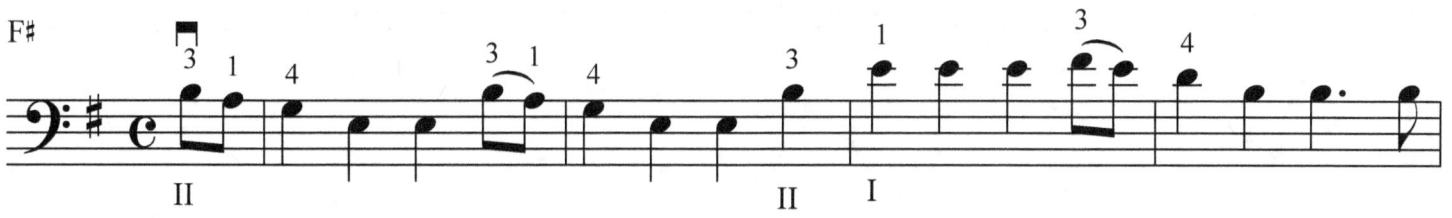

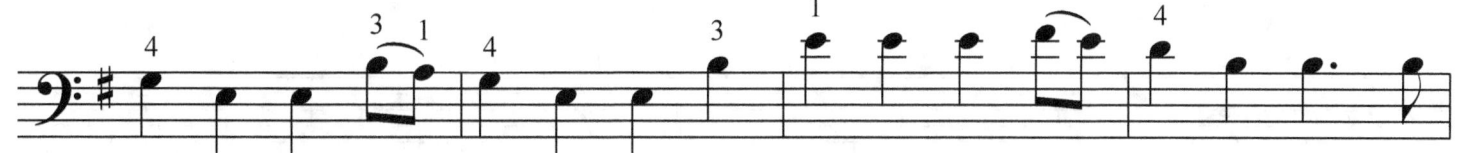

Third Finger E on the G string

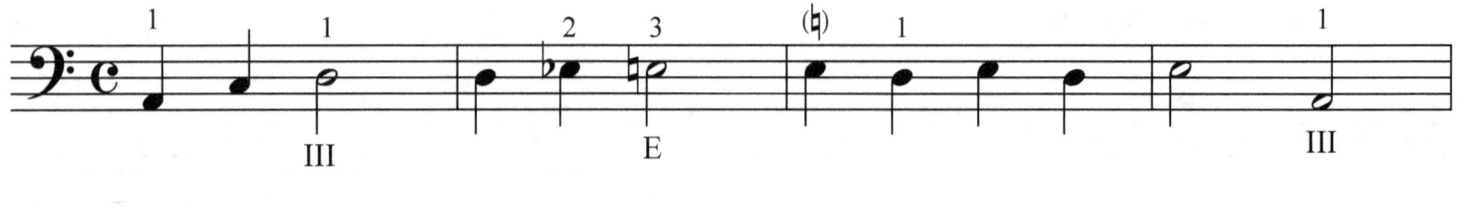

Third Finger A on the C string

Across Strings in Fourth Position

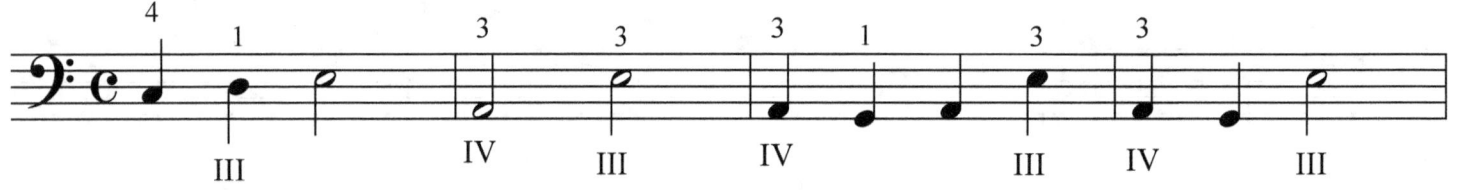

Exercise for The Distant Mountains

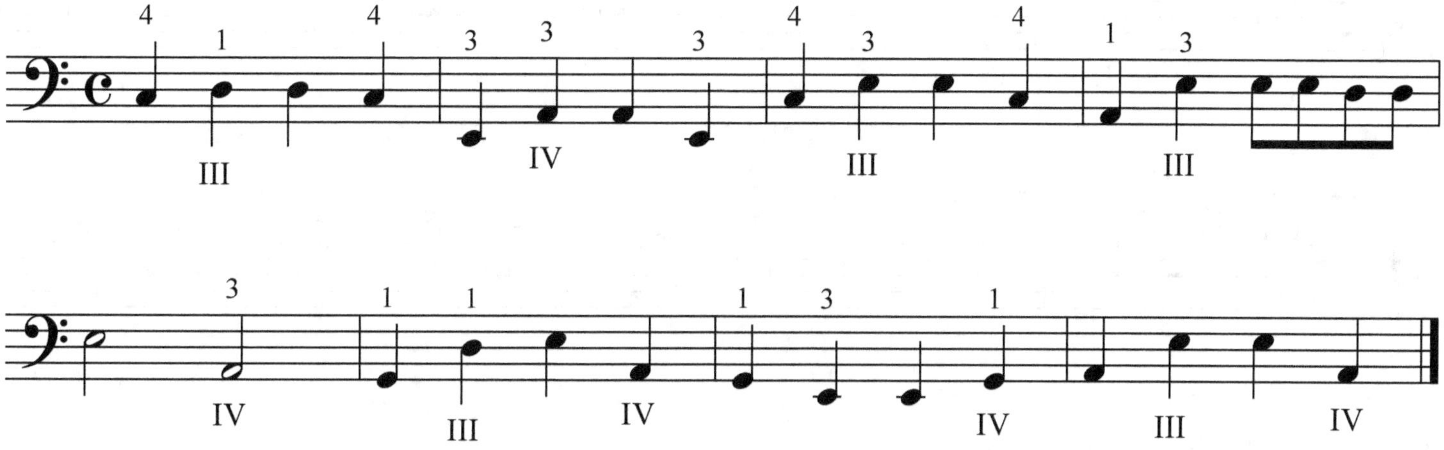

The Distant Mountains

Harvey

E, F♯, and G on the A string

A, B, and C on the D string

Across Strings in Fourth Position

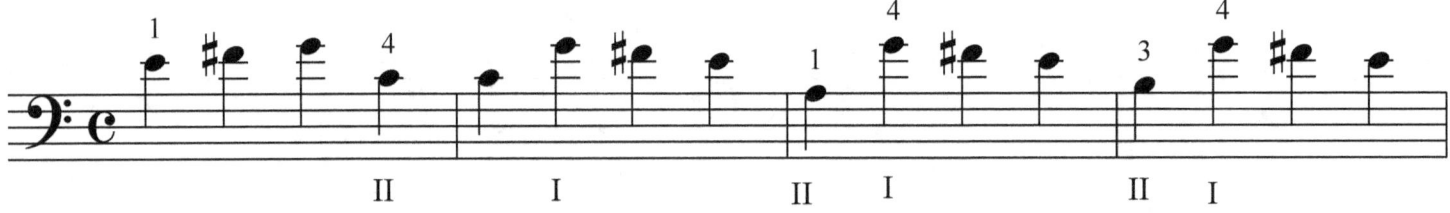

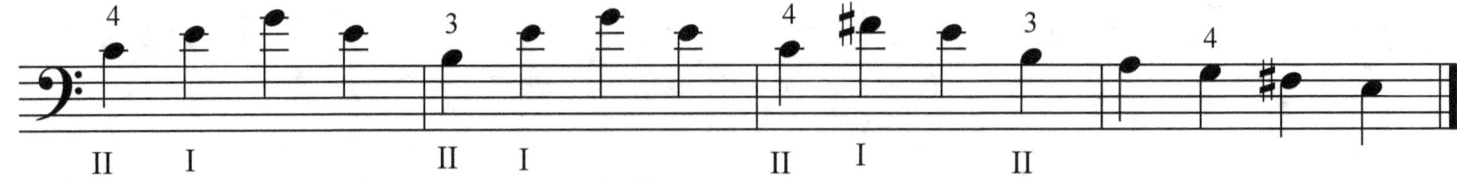

Fourth Position Study Method for Cello

Brighton Camp

Trad., arr. Harvey

©2018 C. Harvey Publications. All Rights Reserved.

Fourth Position Study Method for Cello

D, E, and F on the G string

G, A, and B♭ on the C string

Across Strings in Fourth Position

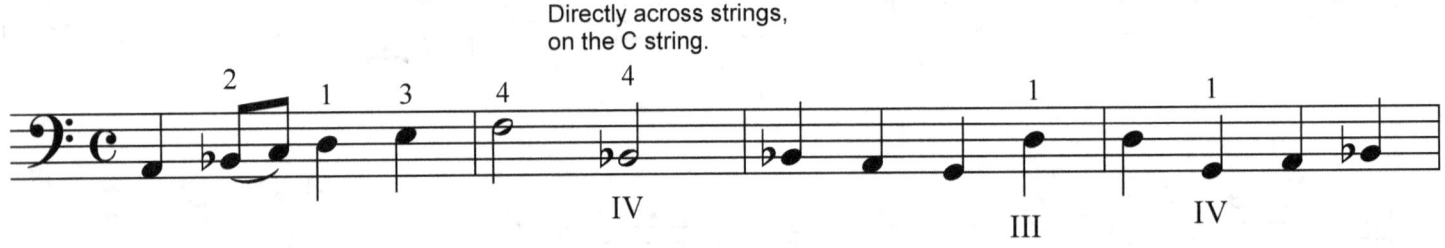

Exercise for Breton Dance Tune

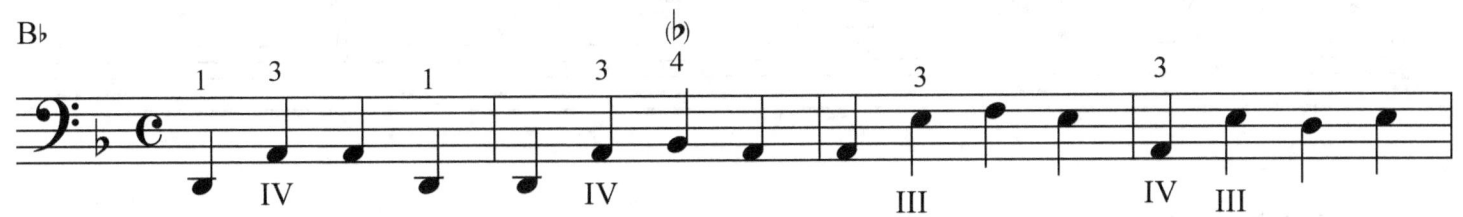

Breton Dance Tune

Trad., arr. Harvey

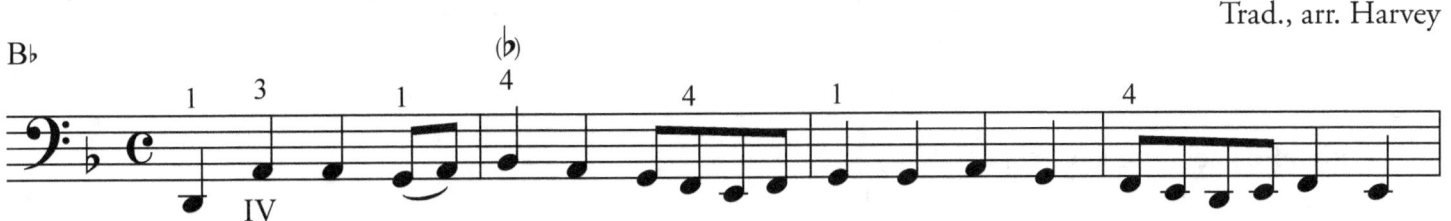

©2018 C. Harvey Publications. All Rights Reserved.

Review the Notes in Fourth Position on the Cello

Fourth Position on the A string

Fourth Position on the D string

Fourth Position on the G string

Fourth Position on the C string

Knowing When to Shift

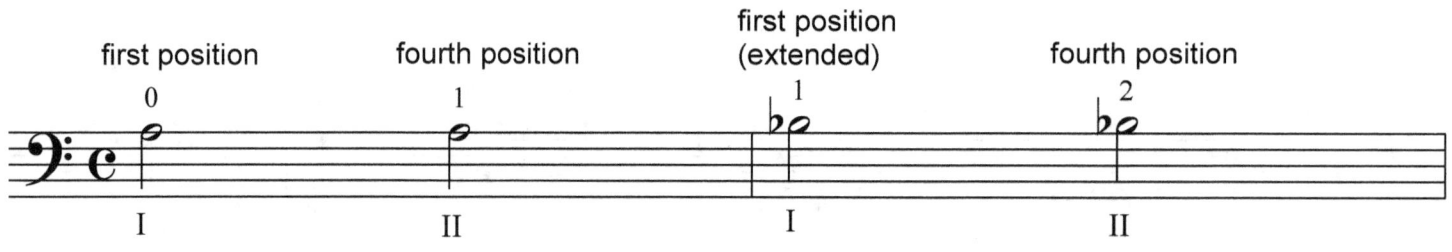

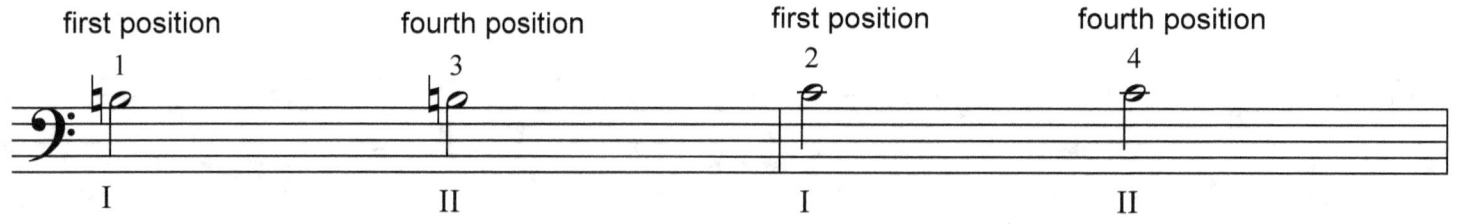

Fourth Position Study Method for Cello

Across Strings in Fourth Position

Slurs and Shifting

When you start playing slurs and shifting, you will hear slides between the notes. This is normal!

As your fingers get stronger and you become more sure of where they are going, the slide sounds will start to disappear. Some slides are kept as part of the cellist's interpretation.

However if you don't want to hear the slides, try these tips:

- Keep your left-hand fingers curved so they shift as cleanly as possible.
- Shift quickly and time the shift so it is exactly between notes (not during one of the notes).
- Keep your bow steady and even; make sure you are not speeding up the bow as you shift.

©2018 C. Harvey Publications. All Rights Reserved.

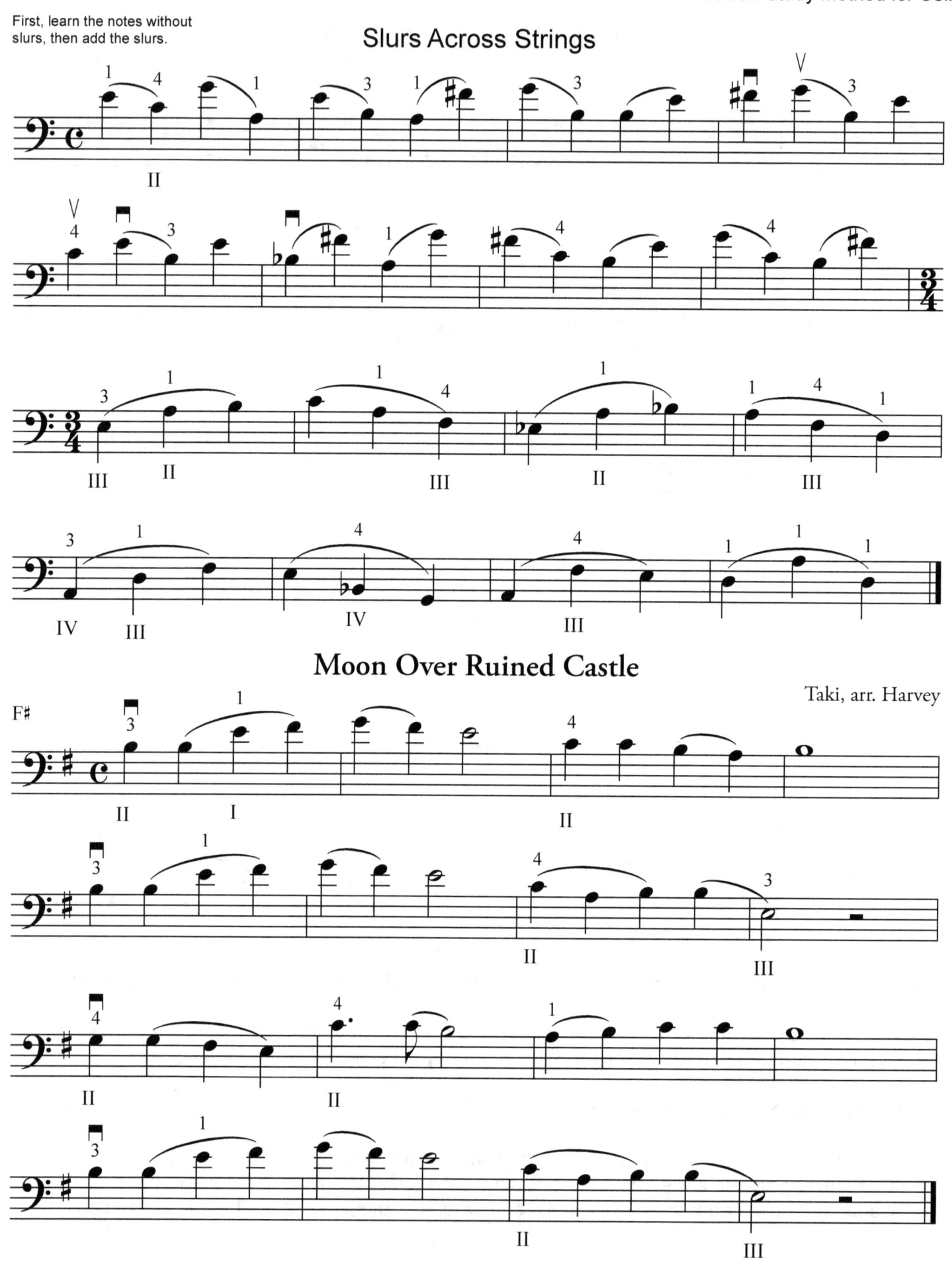

Fourth Position Study Method for Cello

Slurs on the A and D strings

Träumerei

Schumann, arr. Harvey

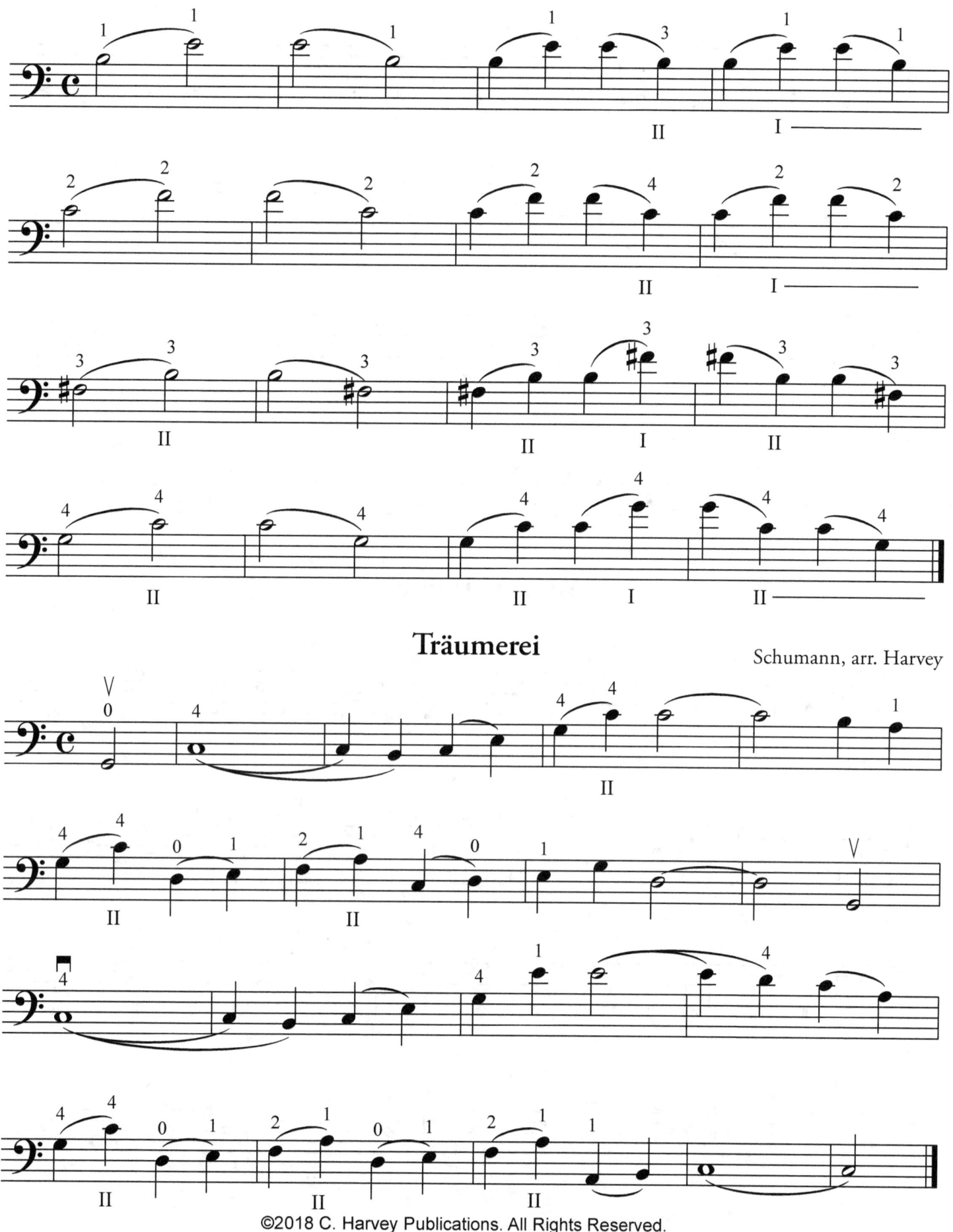

Slurs on the G and C strings

Andante Cantabile

Tchaikovsky, arr. Harvey

Fourth Position Study Method for Cello
35

Finger Exercise with 2nd and 3rd Finger

Supplemental fourth position books available from www.learnstrings.com:
Fourth Position Pieces for the Cello, CHPD16
Fourth Position Shifting for the Cello, CHPD12
Fourth Position Finger Exercises for the Cello, CHPD07

©2018 C. Harvey Publications. All Rights Reserved.

Playing in G Major

Lullaby

Brahms, arr. Harvey

Fourth Position Study Method for Cello

37

Playing in C Major

C Major Etude

©2018 C. Harvey Publications. All Rights Reserved.

The Mid-String Harmonics

A harmonic is a note that you can play on the cello by resting the finger on the string very lightly and **not pressing down**.

Directly above fourth position is a note that can be played either normally (pressed down on the string) or as a **harmonic** (finger resting lightly on the string).

In this book, we will learn this note as a harmonic. For work on the same note pressed down (which would be in cello fifth position), see *Fifth Position for the Cello* or *Fifth Position Preparatory Studies for the Cello*.

Harmonics only work if your finger is in the correct place; if you are having trouble with the harmonic, try moving into position more precisely.

The harmonic note we are learning now is in the middle of the string, between the nut and the bridge. The note is one octave (eight notes) above the open string and has the same name as the open string that it's on: A on the A string, D on the D string, G on the G string, and C on the C string.

You will know when to play a harmonic in this book when you see $\genfrac{}{}{0pt}{}{3}{0}$ over a note.

The "3" in this finger number tells you to use third finger to play the harmonic. All other fingers should be up in the air (not touching the string.)

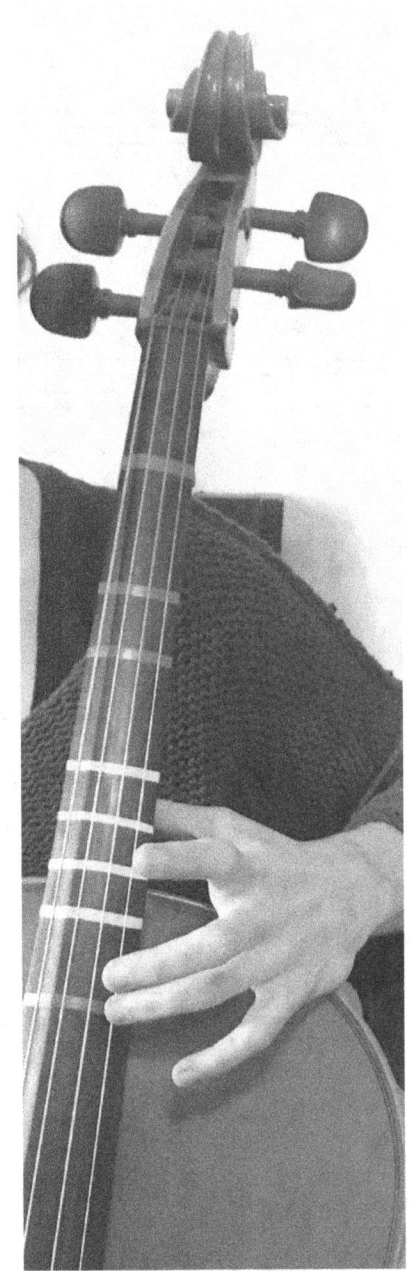

Form Tips

- Keep your left hand and arm high enough (out to the side) that you don't get stuck behind the side of the cello. This will make it easier to shift to the harmonic.
- Curve the fingers of the left hand when you are in fourth position.
- You may straighten the third finger slightly as you use it to reach past fourth position and play the harmonic.

Natural harmonics won't work if more than one finger is on the string at a time. Pick the non-playing fingers up in the air.

Fourth Position Study Method for Cello

The note is A and it is the mid-string harmonic on the A string.

The note is D and it is the mid-string harmonic on the D string.

The note is G and it is the mid-string harmonic on the G string.

The note is C and it is the mid-string harmonic on the C string.

To test whether you are in the correct place to play the harmonic, try pressing the harmonic note down on the string (written as "3"). If you are in the correct place, the harmonic and the regular (pressed down) notes will sound at the same pitch.

The "A" Harmonic on the A string

The "D" Harmonic on the D string

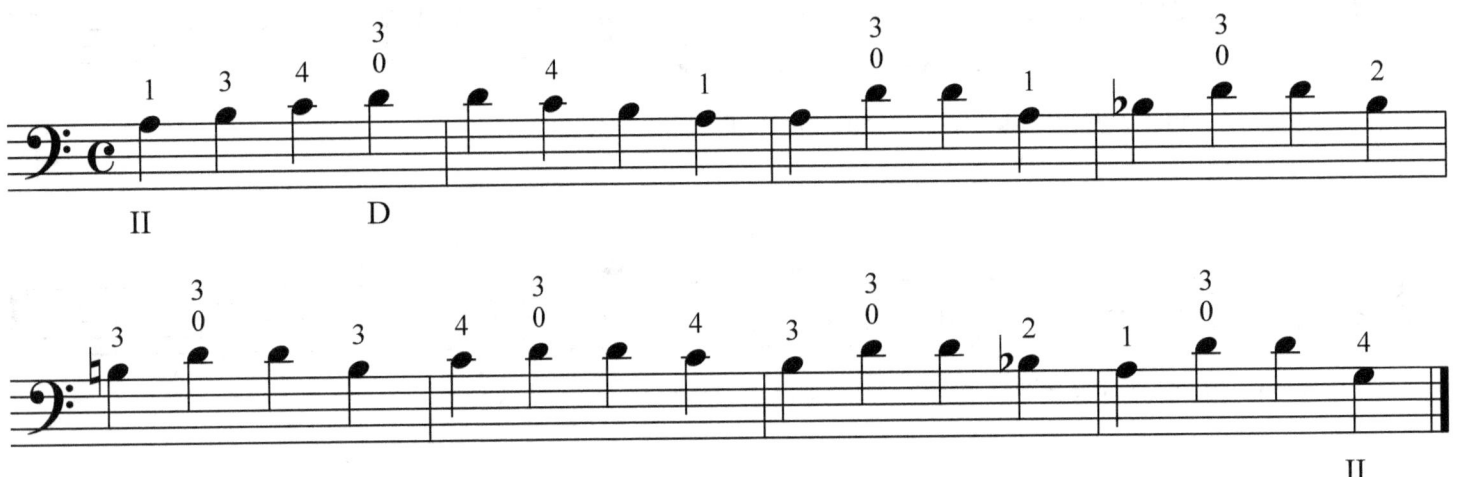

Across Strings to Harmonics

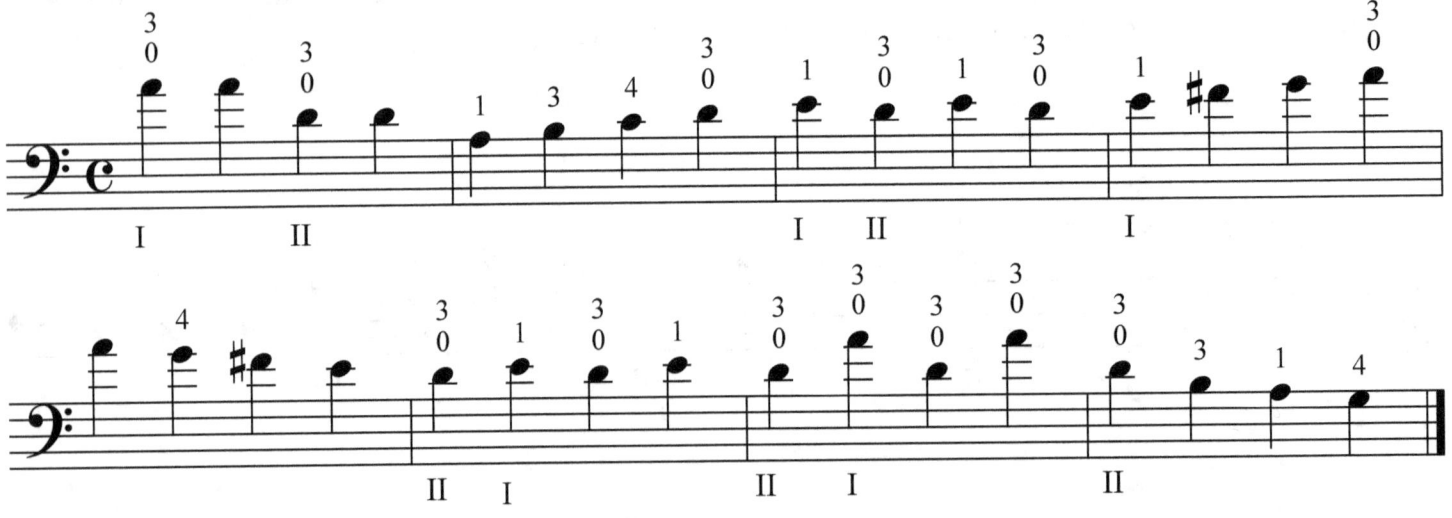

Fourth Position Study Method for Cello

Exercise for Charlie is My Darling

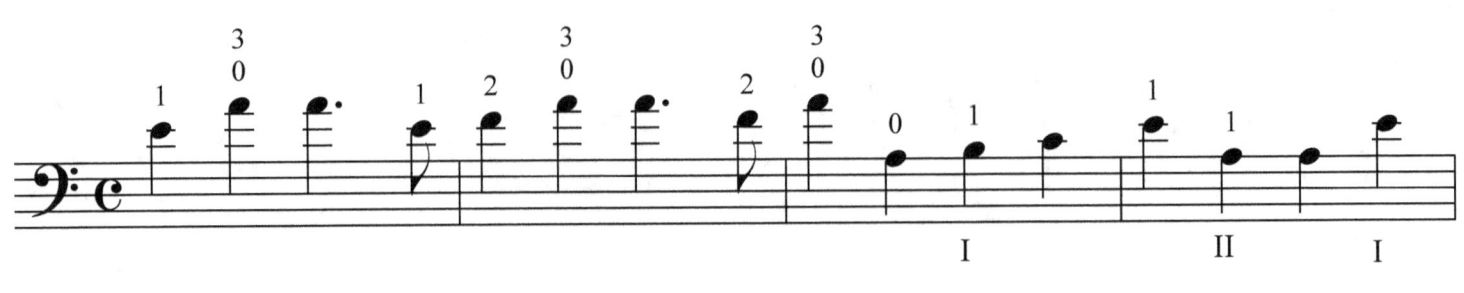

Charlie is My Darling

Trad., arr. Harvey

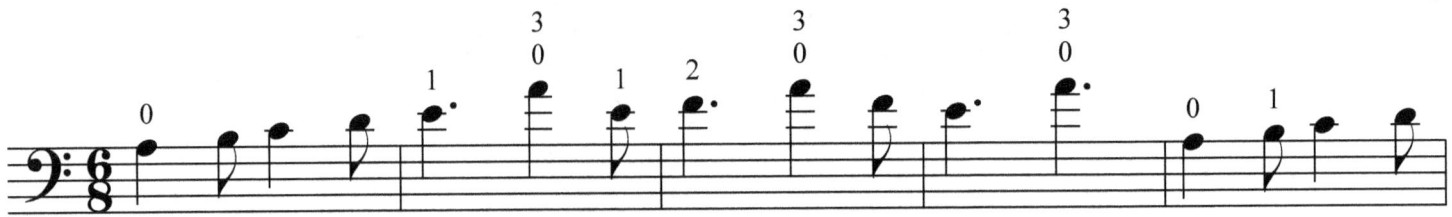

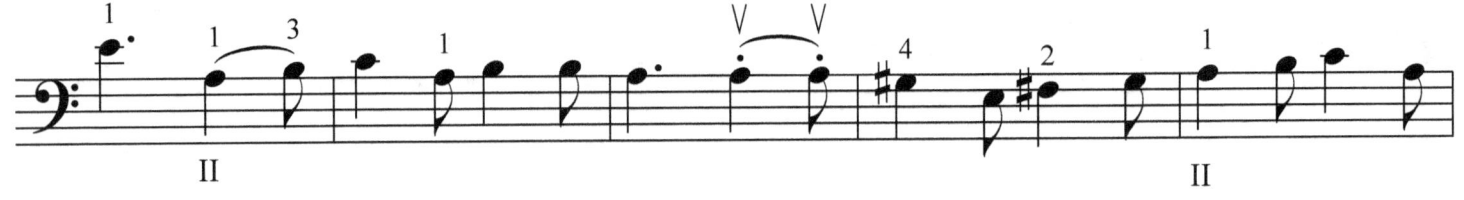

Fourth Position Study Method for Cello
43

Exercise for The Sprig of Shillelah

The Sprig of Shillelah

Trad., arr. Harvey

©2018 C. Harvey Publications. All Rights Reserved.

The "G" Harmonic on the G string

The "C" Harmonic on the C string

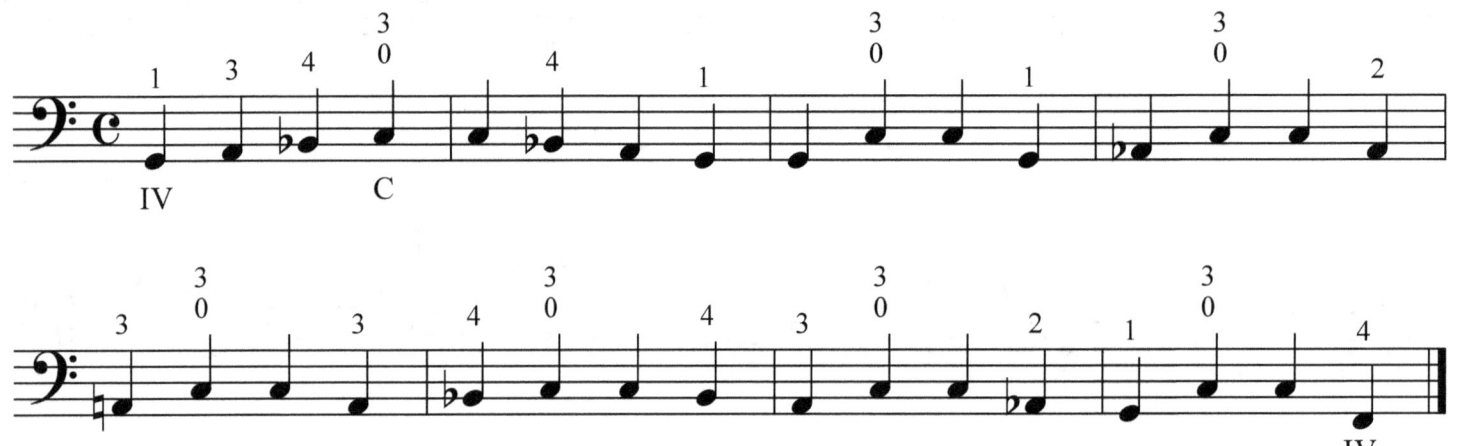

Across Strings to Harmonics

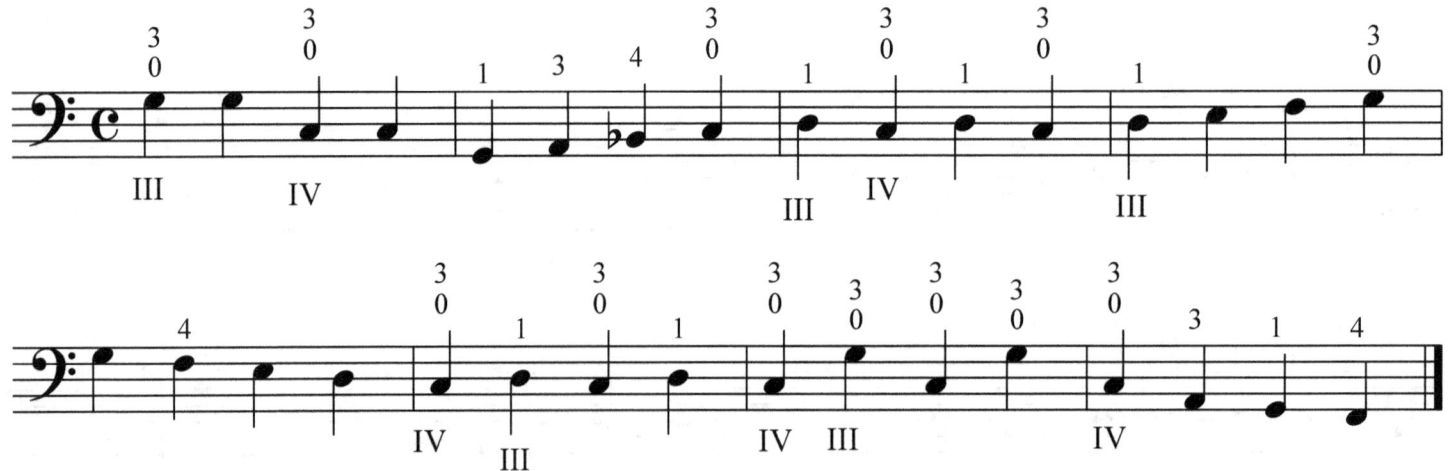

©2018 C. Harvey Publications. All Rights Reserved.

Russian Hymn

Trad., arr. Harvey

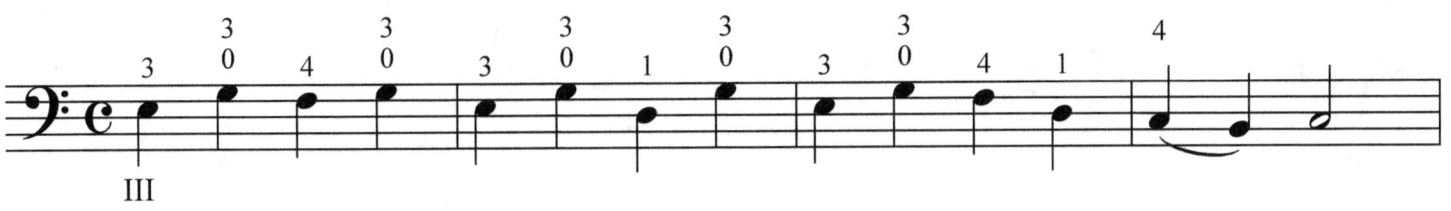

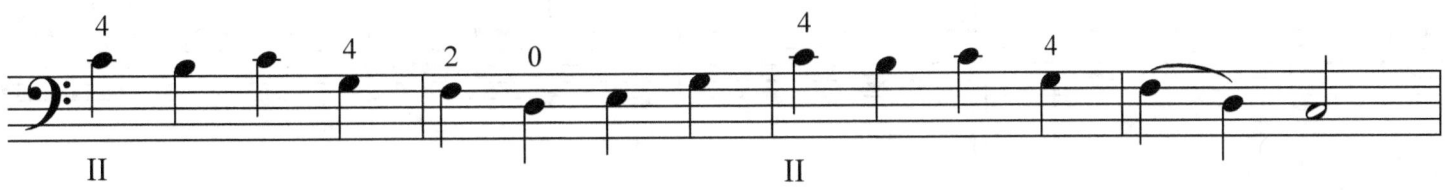

German Folk Tune

Trad., arr. Harvey

Exercise for Paddy Bull's Expedition

B♭, E♭

Paddy Bull's Expedition

Trad., arr. Harvey

B♭, E♭

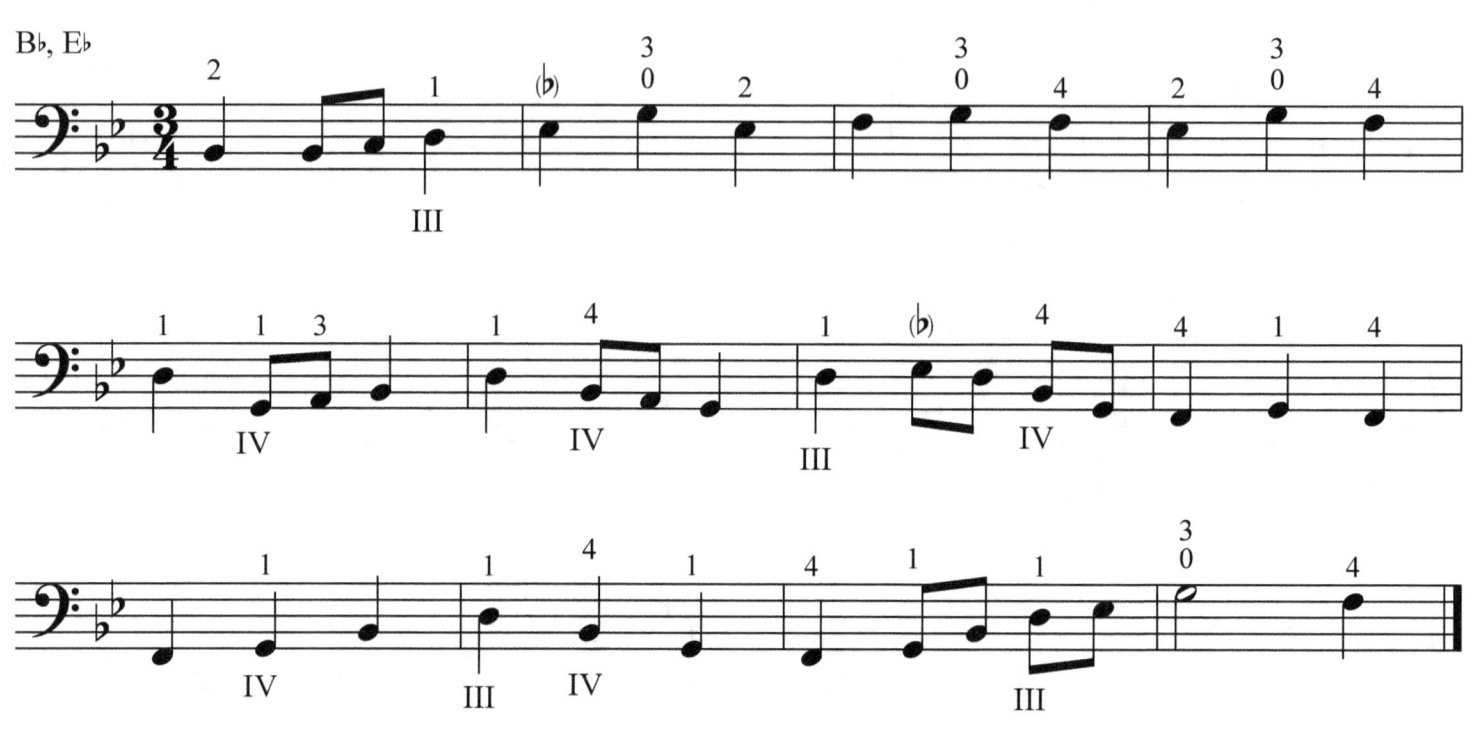

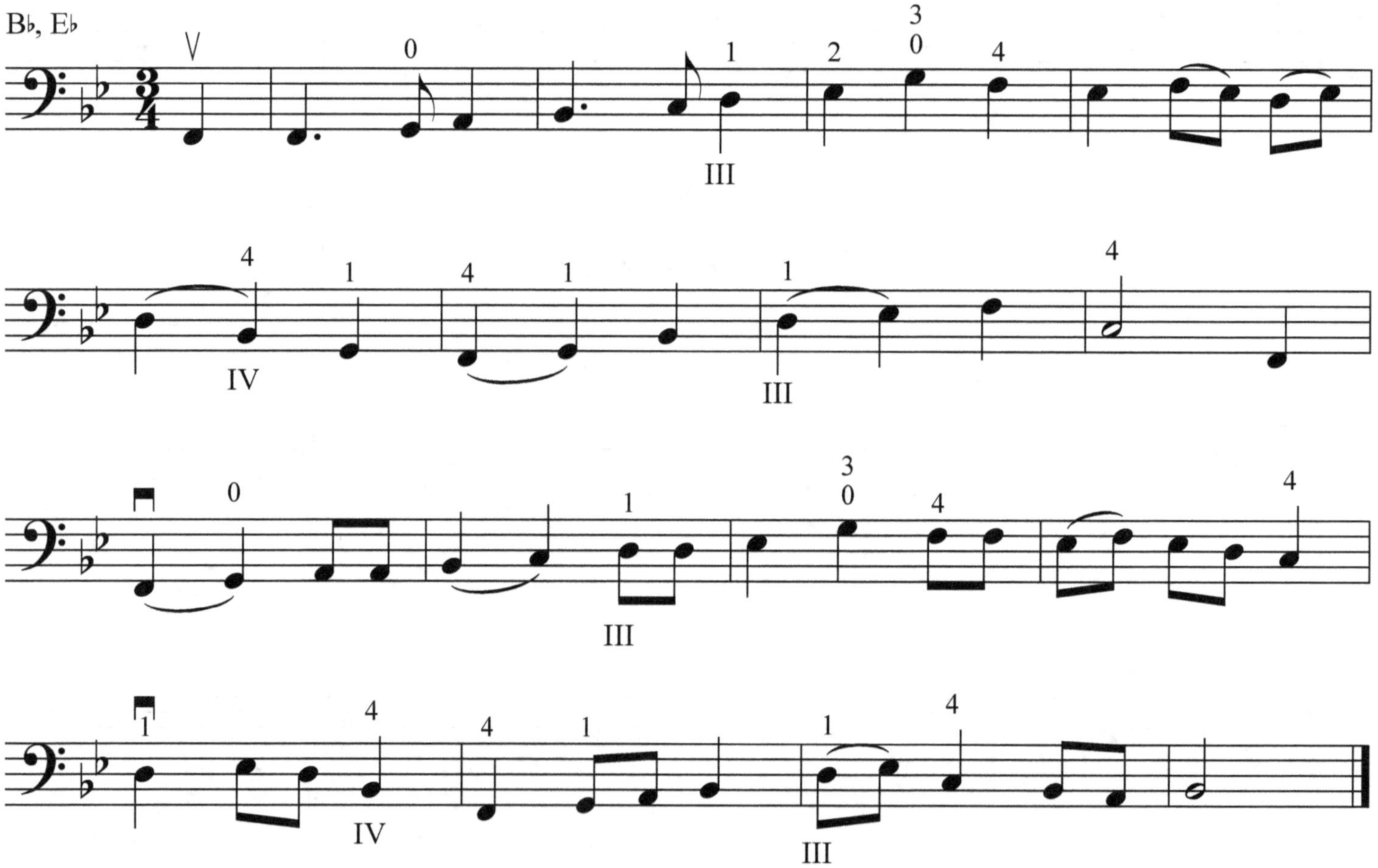

Fourth Position Study Method for Cello

Harmonics Across Strings

Can-Can

Offenbach, arr. Harvey

Extending Back to First Finger Flat

Extensions let you reach even more notes in fourth position.

A half step is the normal space between 1st and 2nd finger (or 2nd and 3rd, or 3rd and 4th finger). Two half steps equal a whole step, which is the normal space between 1st and 3rd finger (or 2nd and 4th finger.) **Reaching a whole step with 1st and 2nd finger is called an extension.**

Extending the 1st finger back one half-step allows you to reach a new note, staying in fourth position instead of shifting to a new position.

To extend back, keep the 2nd, 3rd, and 4th fingers in their regular fourth position places. Reach back one half-step with the 1st finger. The 1st finger will be on a new note, while the rest of the fingers are on their usual notes.

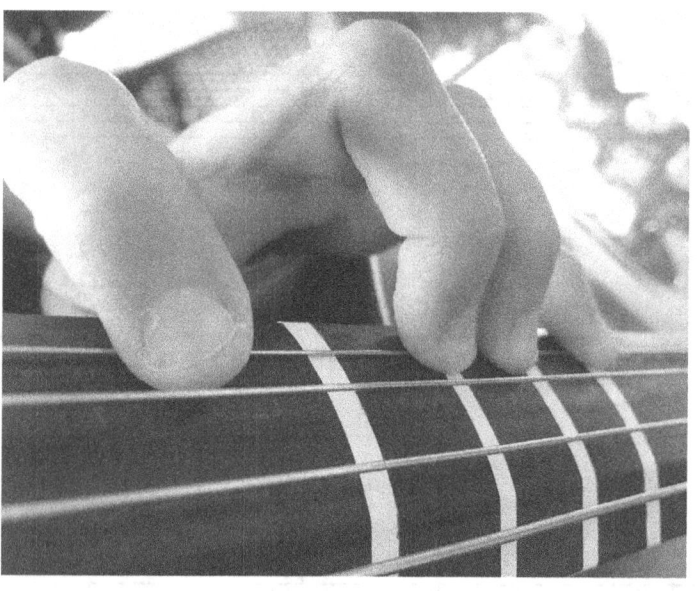

Form Tips

- Your finger might touch the string using a different part of the fingertip while extending.
- Keep your left wrist straight and the left arm out to the side.
- Keep the thumb up as far under the cello neck as possible.
- Take breaks frequently when you are learning extensions.

Stretch back gently; don't force your hand to reach. A good extension technique comes with practice over a long period of time. Forcing your hand to stretch to the point where you feel pain could result in injury.

©2018 C. Harvey Publications. All Rights Reserved.

Fourth Position Study Method for Cello

First Finger, Extended Back, Across Strings

Closed and Extended Fourth Position

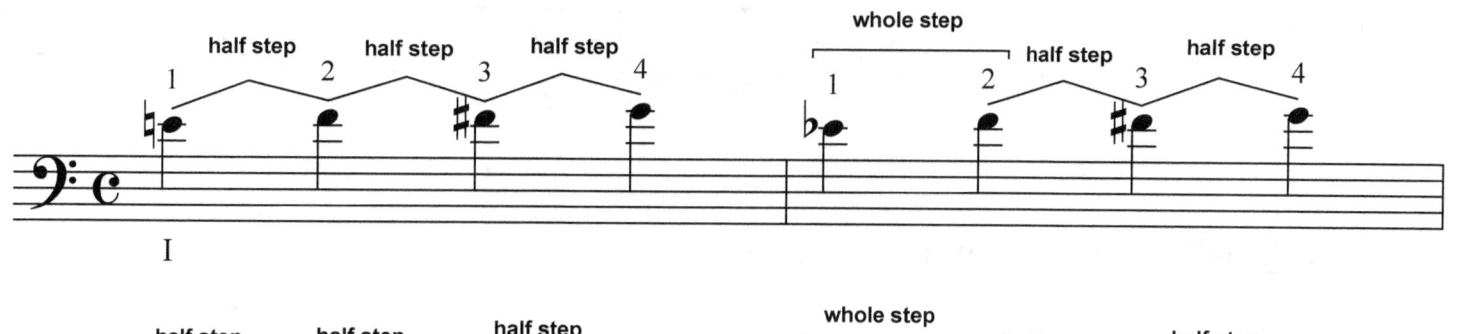

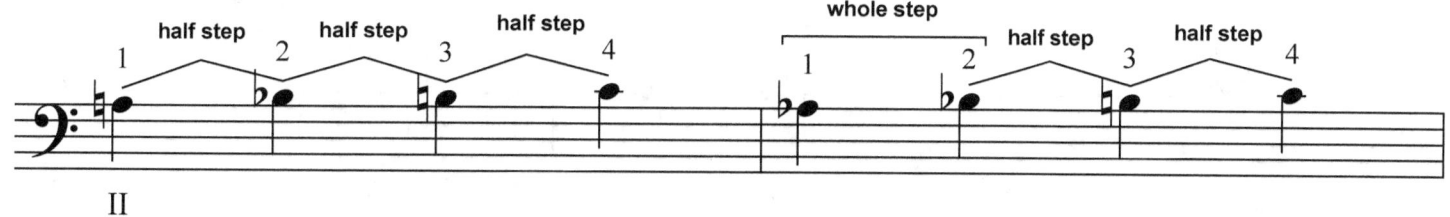

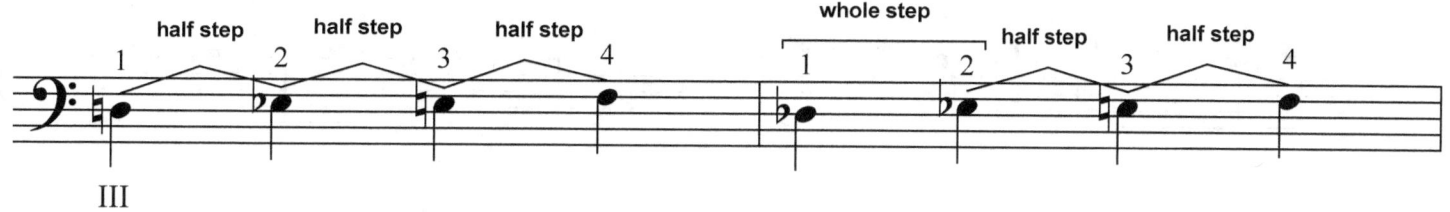

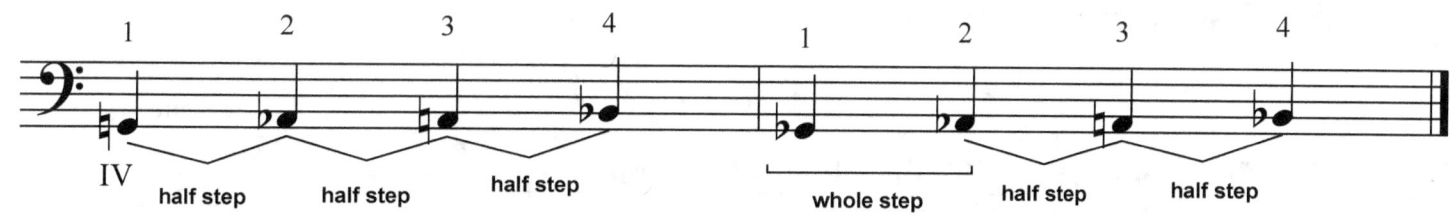

How Extended Fourth Position is Related to First Position

©2018 C. Harvey Publications. All Rights Reserved.

Extending Back to Reach E♭ on the A string

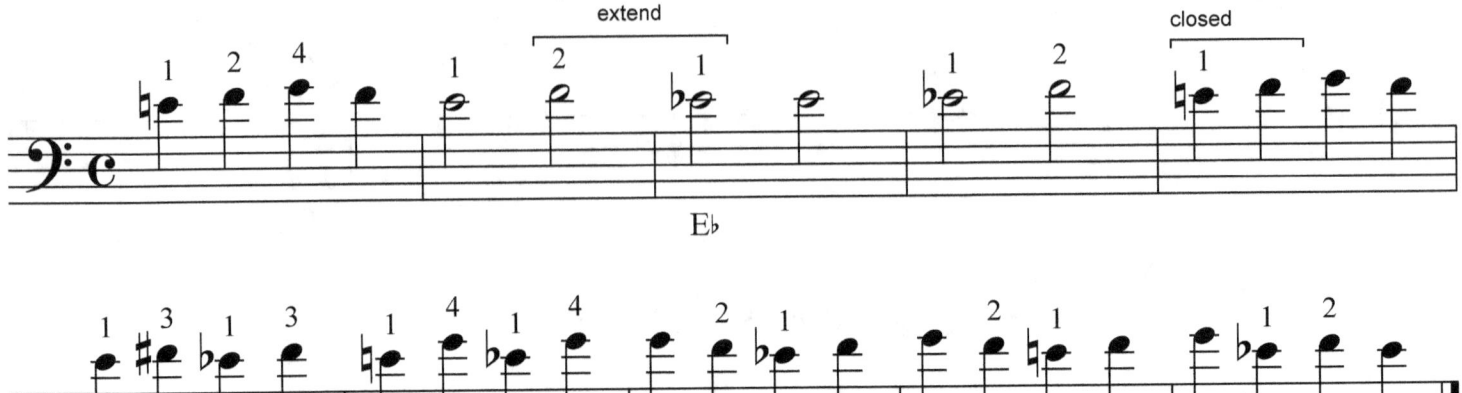

Extending Back to Reach A♭ on the D string

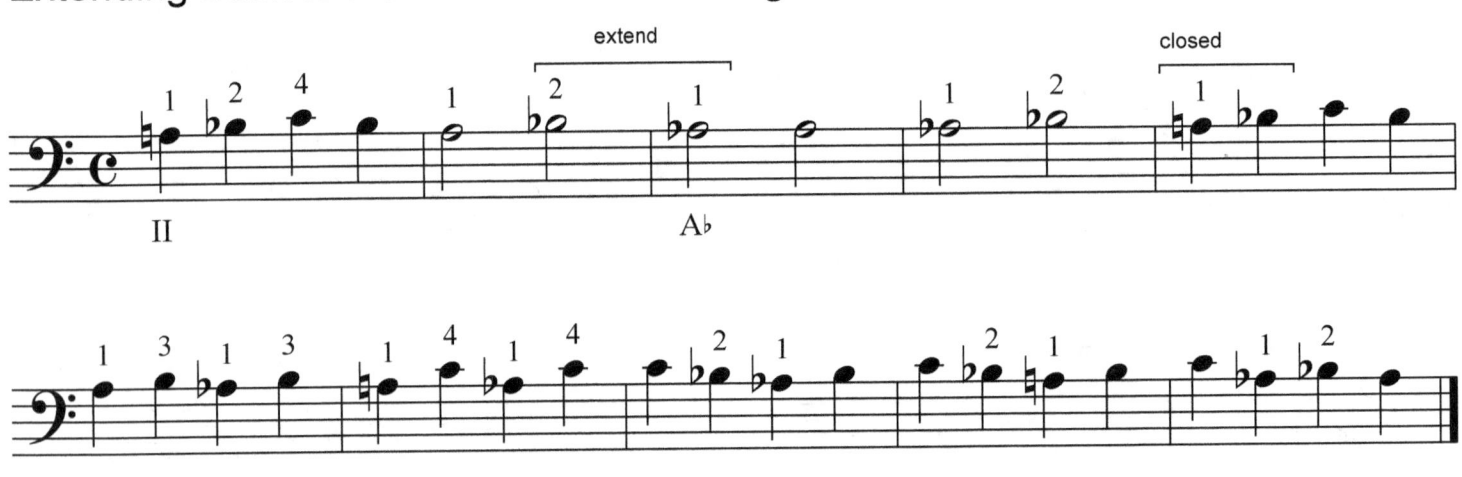

Extending Back Across Strings

Fourth Position Study Method for Cello

Extending Back to Reach D♭ on the G string

Extending Back to Reach G♭ on the C string

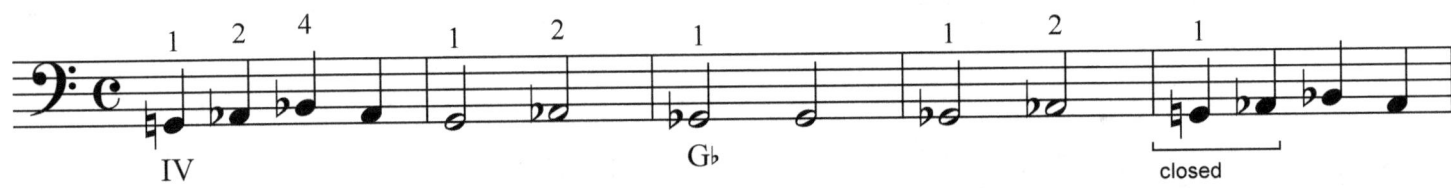

Extending Back Across Strings

©2018 C. Harvey Publications. All Rights Reserved.

Fourth Position Study Method for Cello

Exercise for Mariner's Lament

Mariner's Lament

Harvey

Exercise for Cumberland Gap

Cumberland Gap

Trad., arr. Harvey

Note: Remain in extended fourth position for this entire piece.

Fourth Position Study Method for Cello

Exercise for Arirang

Arirang

Trad., arr. Harvey

Bb, Eb, Ab, Db

Note: Remain in extended fourth position for this entire piece.

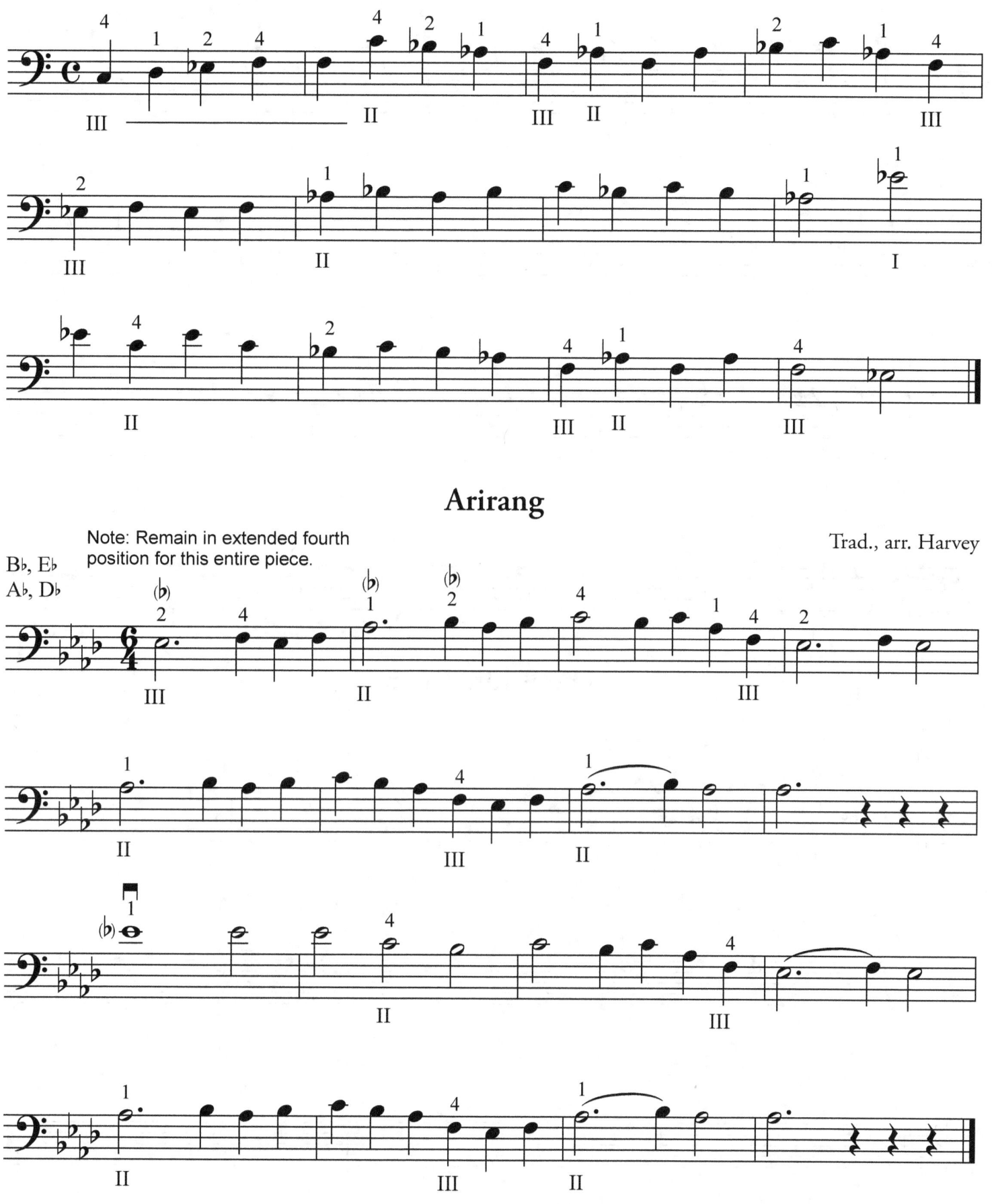

©2018 C. Harvey Publications. All Rights Reserved.

Shifting Back from Extended Fourth Position on the A and D strings.

The White Birch

Trad., arr. Harvey

Fourth Position Study Method for Cello

Shifting Back from Extended Fourth Position on the G and C strings.

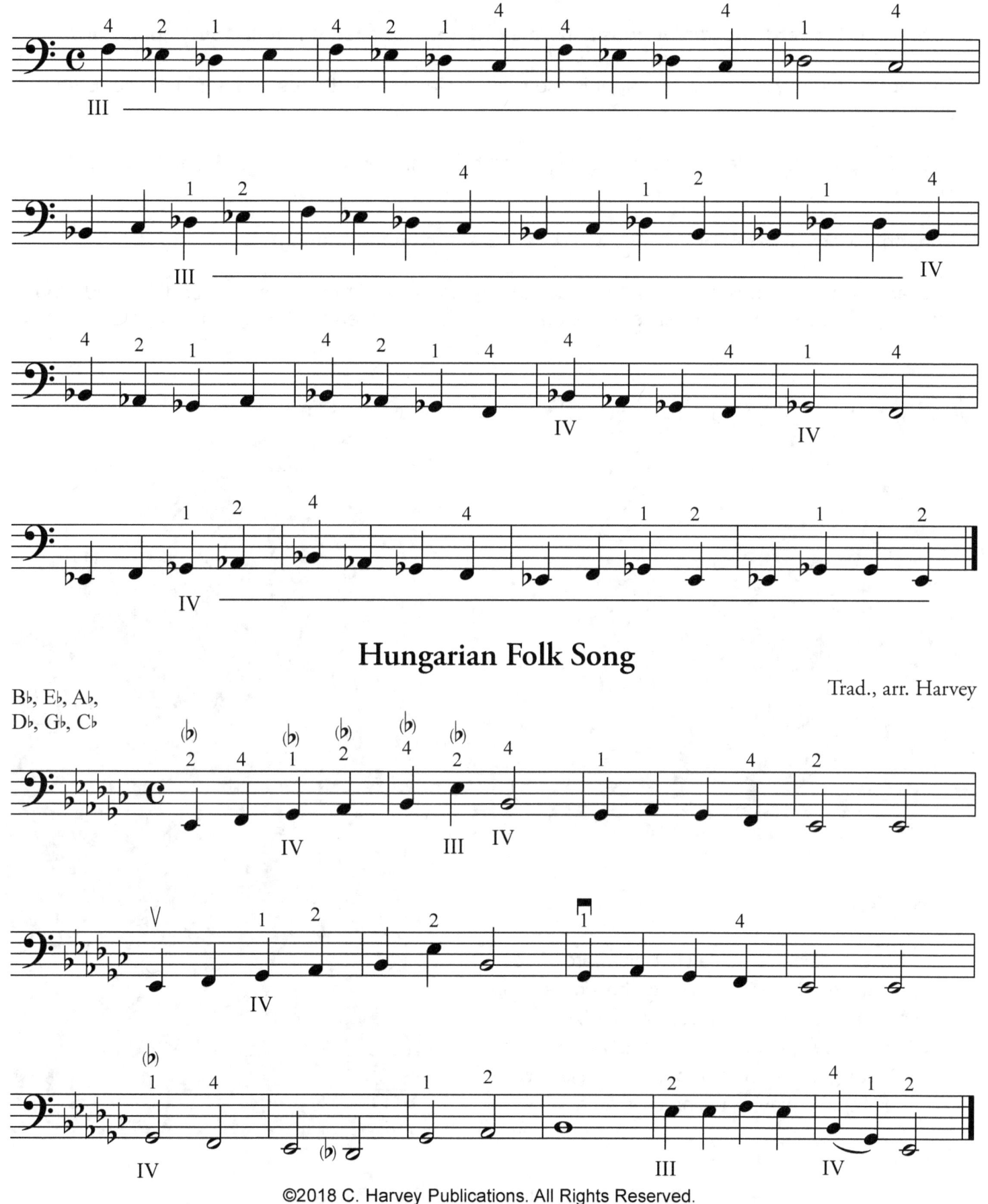

Hungarian Folk Song

Trad., arr. Harvey

Extending Forward to a Fourth Finger Sharp

Extending forward allows you to reach an extra note on each string in fourth position.

To extend forward, keep the 1st finger in the regular place in fourth position (for instance, E on the A string).

Extend 2nd finger to play the note usually played by 3rd finger (for instance, F-sharp on the A string).

The 4th finger will naturally fall 1/2 step higher (G-sharp on the A string).

The actual extension is between 1st and 2nd fingers. This eliminates stress on the hands that would occur if we extended between the 2nd and 3rd or between the 3rd and 4th fingers.

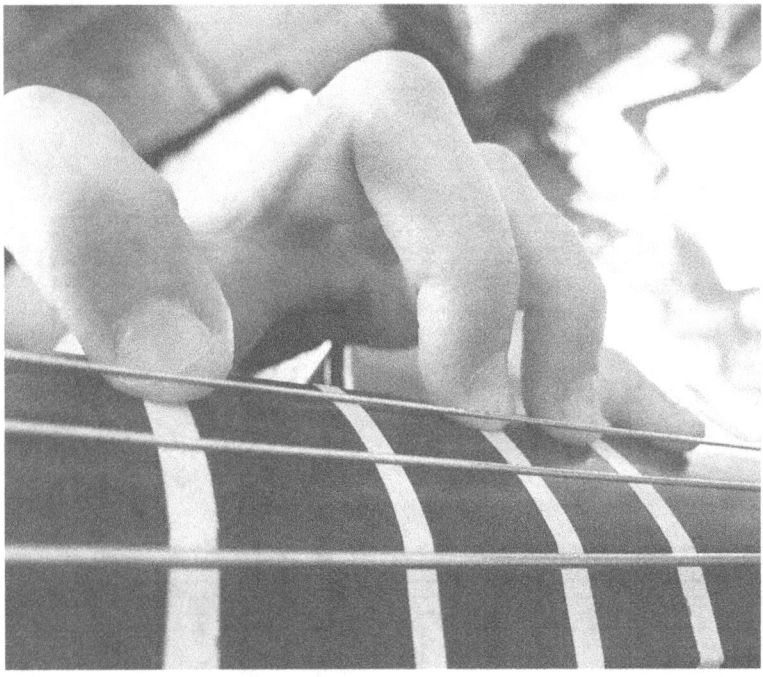

Form Tips

- This extension is somewhat awkward. Focus on keeping the left arm out to the side so you can reach the notes as well as possible.
- Don't force the extension. Instead, focus on general good form (arm out to the side, wrist straight) and playing the notes in tune.

Fourth Position Study Method for Cello

Closed and Extended Fourth Position

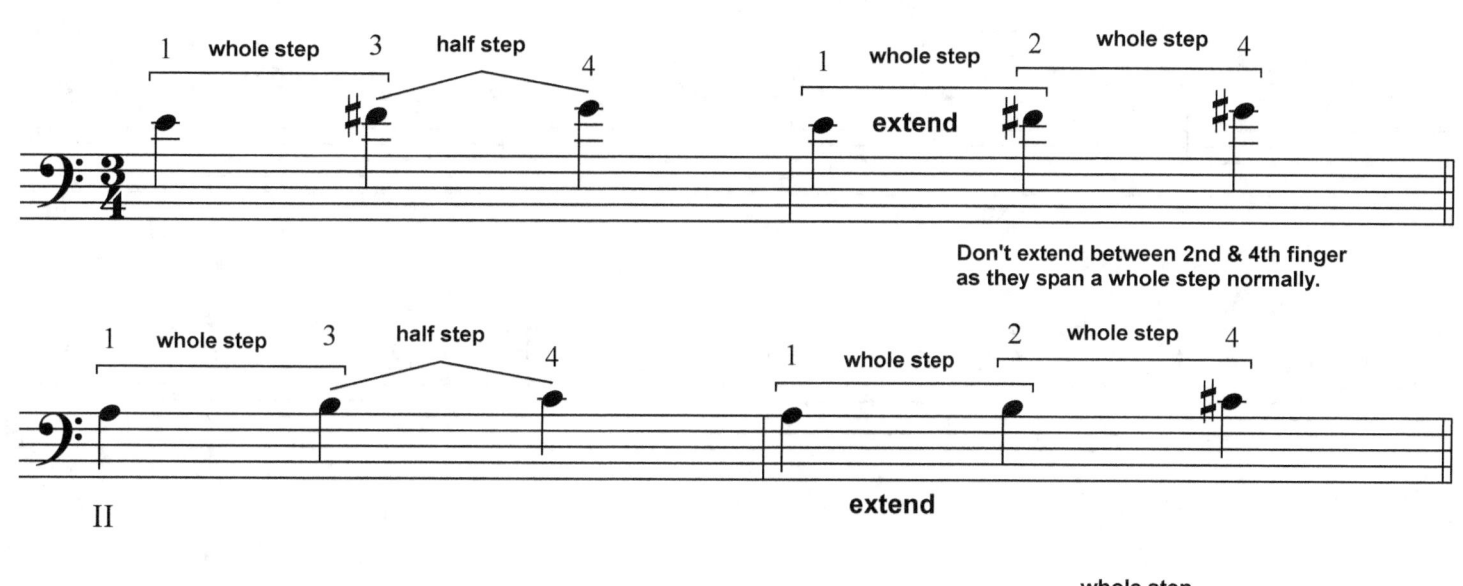

Fourth Finger, Extended, Across Strings

Using 3rd Finger in Extended Fourth Position

Extending Forward to Reach G# on the A string

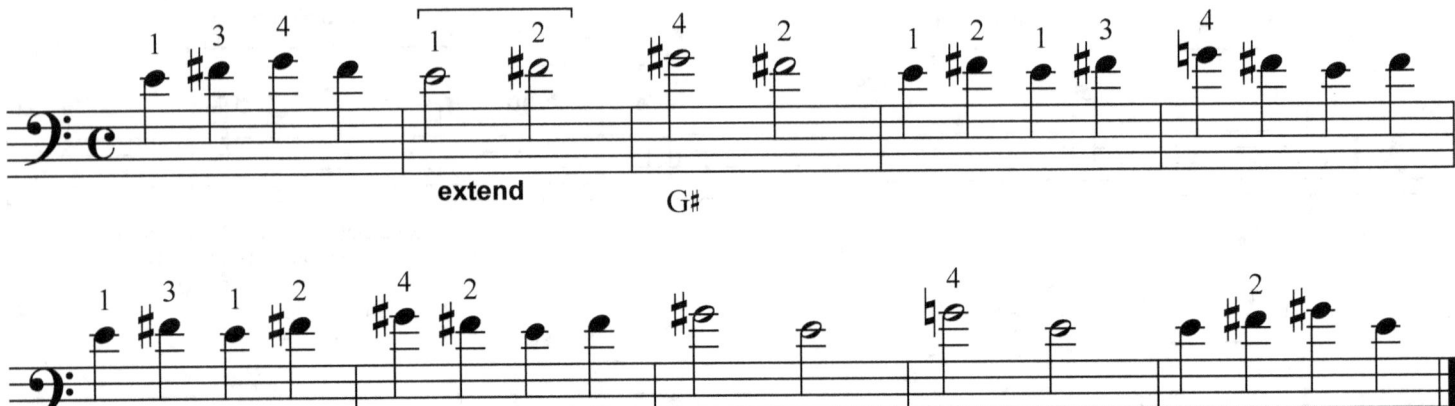

Extending Forward to Reach C# on the D string

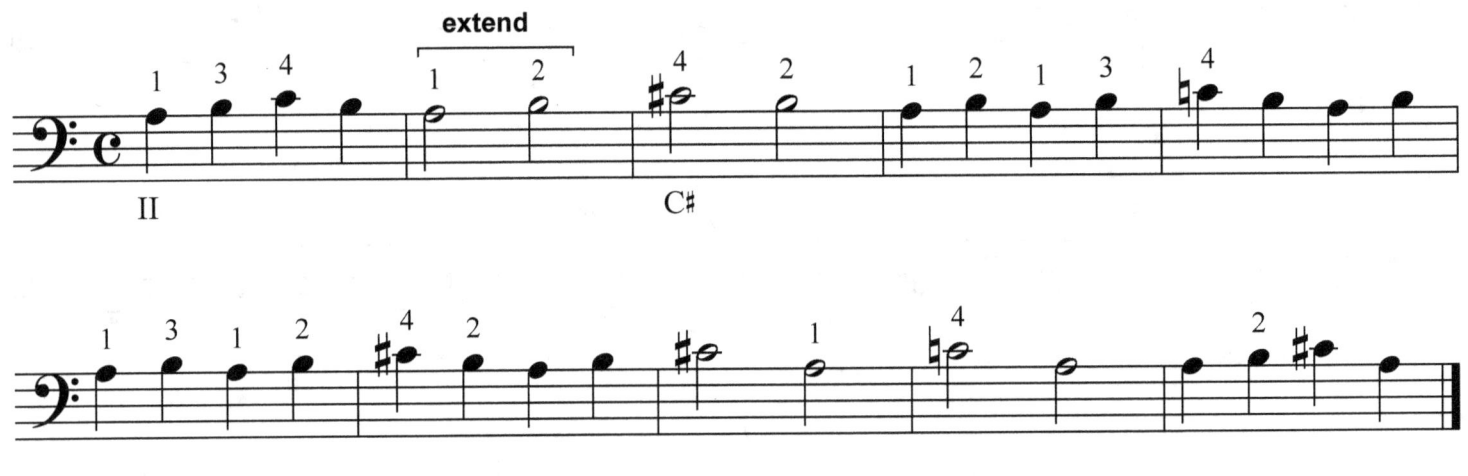

Extending Forward Across Strings

Drill Ye Tarriers

Trad., arr. Harvey

Falling Down

Harvey

Fourth Position Study Method for Cello

Exercise for Old Paint

Old Paint

Trad., arr. Harvey

Fourth Position Study Method for Cello

Exercise for Spring Rain

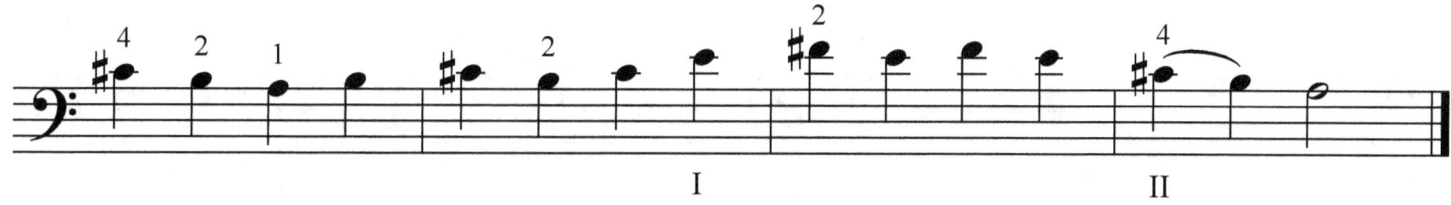

Spring Rain

Harvey

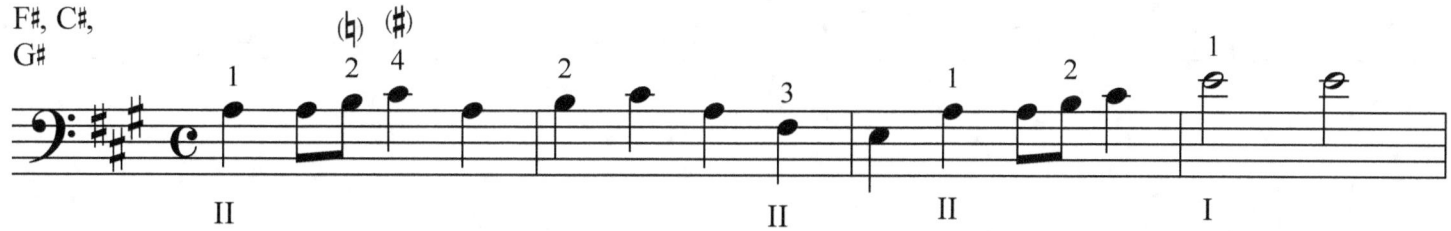

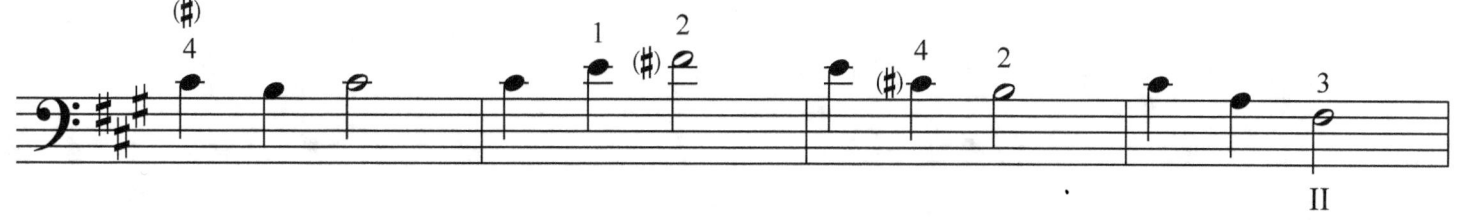

©2018 C. Harvey Publications. All Rights Reserved.

Extending Forward to Reach F♯ on the G string

Extending Forward to Reach B♮ on the C string

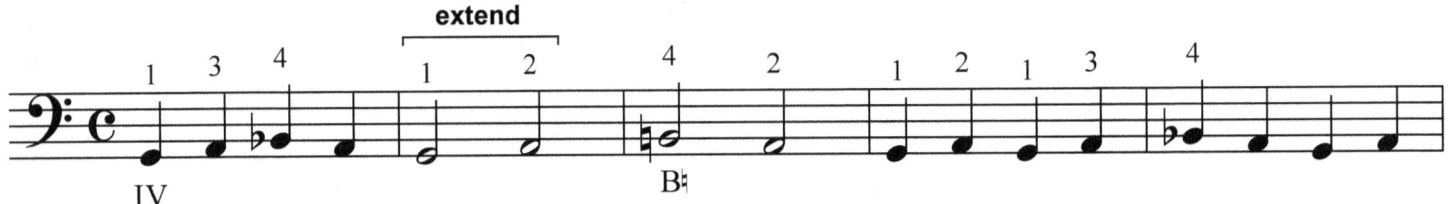

Extending Forward Across Strings

Greensleeves

Trad., arr. Harvey

Theme from 'William Tell'

Rossini, arr. Harvey

Shifting To and From Extended Positions

Vive La Compagnie

Benteen, arr. Harvey

Fourth Position Study Method for Cello

Extending Across Strings

Flow Gently, Sweet Afton

Spilman, arr. Harvey

Double Stops on the A and D strings

Double Stops on the D and G strings

Yankee Doodle

Trad., arr. Harvey

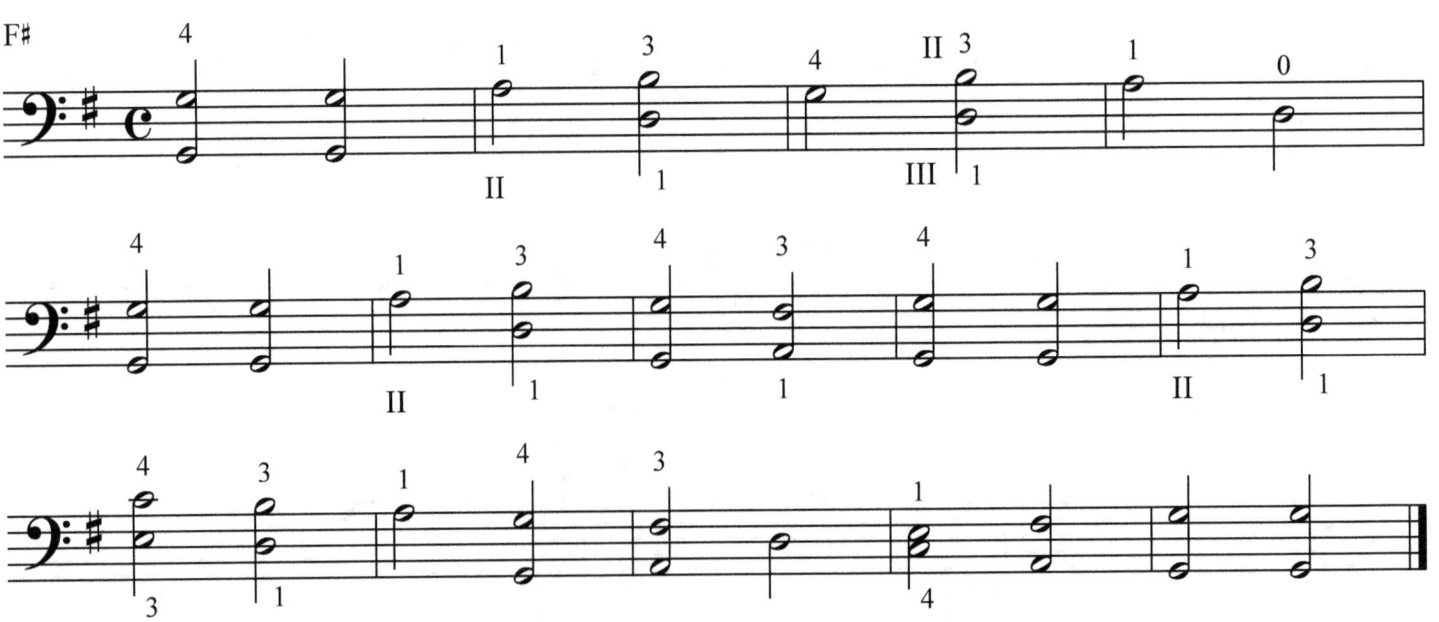

Au Claire de la Lune

Trad., arr. Harvey

Double Stops on the G and C strings

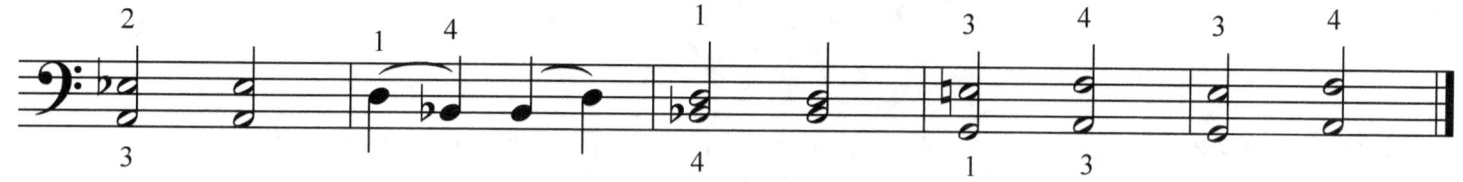

Old Joe Clark

Trad., arr. Harvey

©2018 C. Harvey Publications. All Rights Reserved.

Building Good Tone in Fourth Position

Good tone, or sound, on the cello comes from having good technical skills and from following these principles:

1. On fingered notes, stop the string completely with the fingers of the left hand. A completely stopped string will be able to vibrate fully. Double stop exercises (see pp. 68-69), and Finger exercises (see pp. 20, 35, or the book *Fourth Position Finger Exercises for the Cello*, CHPD07) can help strengthen the fingers and improve your tone.
2. Catch the string with the bow to make it start vibrating. When you pull the bow to play a note, continue to make the string vibrate. The more the string vibrates, the better the tone will be.
3. Play at the correct soundpoint. Imagine 5 lanes, or soundpoints, between the fingerboard and the bridge. Soundpoint #1 is where you should play fast separate bows. As the bow pressure increases, move closer to the bridge (towards Soundpoints #2-5.) As the bow speed decreases, move closer to the bridge (towards Soundpoints #2-5.) And as the notes go higher (higher positions), move closer to the bridge (towards Soundpoints #2-5.) Fourth position is usually played with the bow at Soundpoints #2-4.

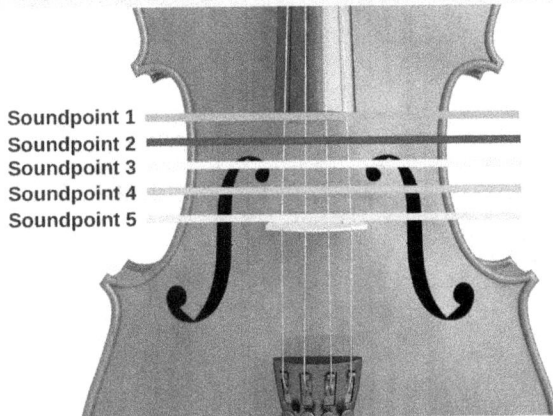

First play the exercise below entirely at Soundpoint 1, with the dynamic ***fortissimo***.
Then play it as written, still at ***fortissimo*** and see how the tone improves.

To get from one soundpoint to another, gradually move up or down as the bow is playing (moving across the strings.)

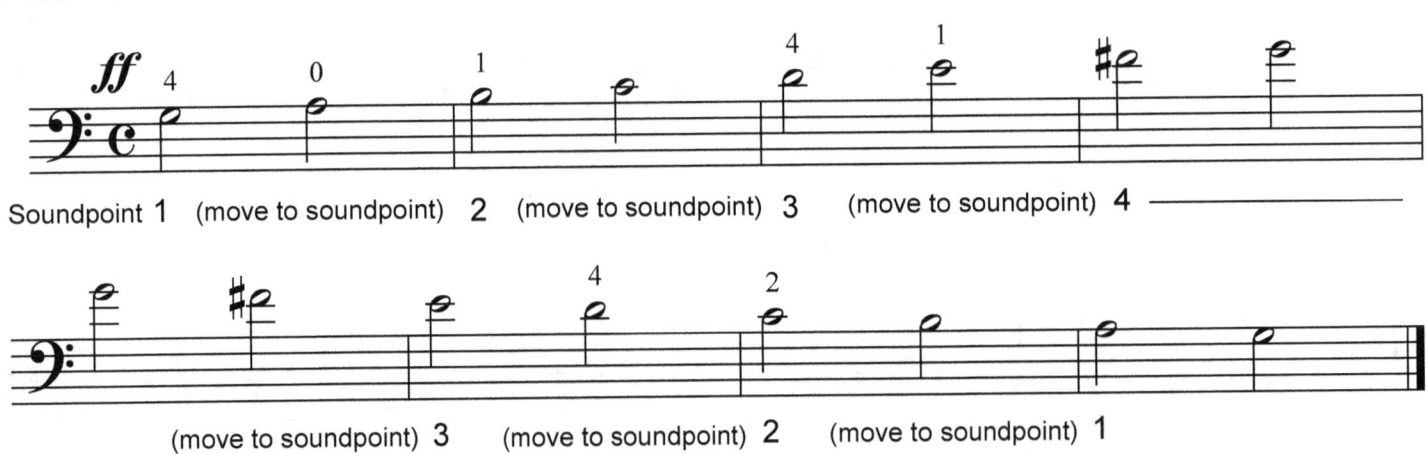

©2018 C. Harvey Publications. All Rights Reserved.

Fourth Position Study Method for Cello

71

First practice this exercises without the dynamics. Then add the dynamics, using slightly narrower, faster vibrato as you crescendo and wider, slower vibrato as you decrescendo.

Vibrato Exercise

Oh Freedom

Traditional, arr. Harvey

©2018 C. Harvey Publications. All Rights Reserved.

Shifting Back 1/2 Step

Excerpt from Sonata in E minor

Romberg, edited Harvey

Fourth Position Study Method for Cello

Shifting Forward 1/2 Step to High Fourth Position

Etude

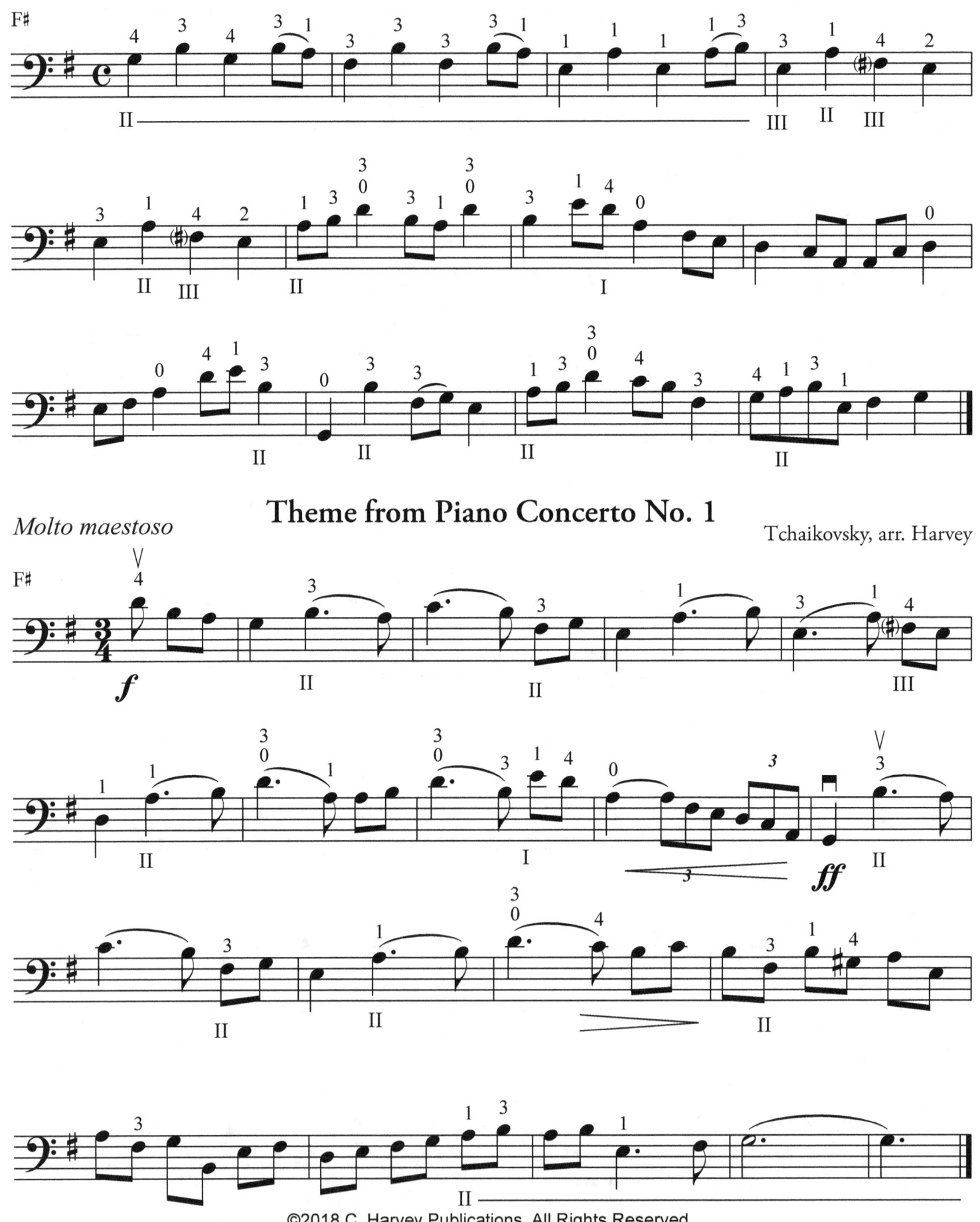

www.ingramcontent.com/pod-product-compliance
Lightning Source LLC
Chambersburg PA
CBHW051422070526
44584CB00023B/3540